BREAKING CRAZY

BREAKING CRAZY

WORKING FROM HOME WITHOUT LOSING YOUR MARBLES

FRIEDA WILEY, PHARMD

STORIES UNLEASHED PUBLISHING, LLC

Find out more about the compiler, Frieda Wiley, PharmD at:
DrFriedaWileyBooks.com
friedawiley.com

Published by Stories Unleashed Publishing, LLC

Originally published under the title "Telecommuting Psychosis: From Surviving to Thriving in Your Pajama Pants." Copyright 2022 by Stories Unleashed Publishing, LLC

ISBN 979-8-9895540-0-3

Typesetting services by BOOKOW.COM

DEDICATION

I dedicate this book to my fourth-grade teacher, Mrs. Donna Powell. Although we got off to a rocky start, as the weeks flew by, we developed a bond that united us in ways we never imagined. Mrs. Powell, I feel your influence every time I sit down to write.

On a fateful Friday about two weeks before the end of the school year, you changed my life with one simple act. You gave me a compilation of poems written by children entitled *Gonna Bake Me a Rainbow Poem* by Peter Sears. On the inside of the book, you'd written a beautiful note encouraging me to keep writing. Earlier that year, the teacher next door, Mrs. Standley, suggested I combine my artistic and writing skills to write and illustrate children's books. She shared a children's book writing contest with me, which the three of us reviewed together. While I submitted nothing, I felt inspired and optimistic about my future career. You both had a tremendous effect on me, but it was you, Mrs. Powell, who planted the first seeds.

I never told you this, but that book you gave me remains among the most prized books in my collection to this day. As a child, I would open it at the end of every school year—not to read the poems—but to read and reread the message you'd written to me. I guess you could say it was a reminder to stay on course and make you proud.

Your message, written in red ink, has since faded to a faint pink, making the letters hard to read. But it doesn't matter. I practically memorized the words. Even now, decades later, the final words from your message still echo in my mind:

"One day, your name will be on the outside of a book as its author."

My eyes welled with tears as you watched me read the last sentence of your message, and I hid them. But those tears remain. In fact, my eyes are tearing as I write this dedication now.

It sure has been one heck of a journey, but I am no longer the insecure, awkward early bloomer who stooped when she walked, and even wore sweaters in the hot Texas sun to hide the physical evidence of puberty. That overgrown fourth grader is long gone. Today, I hold my head up proudly and stand tall; you had a lot to do with that.

Thank you from the bottom of my heart for challenging and supporting me, and for planting a seed that has finally begun to bloom. I could not have done it without you. Here's to the first of my many published books.

And by the way, the children's books are on the way, too.

Frieda Yvonne Eunice Wiley, PharmD

"Hear counsel, and receive instruction,
that thou mayest be wise in thy latter end."

–Proverbs 19:20 (*King James Version*)

Disclaimer

The purpose of this publication is to provide both anecdotal information based on the writer's personal and professional experiences and supplement it with evidence-based research to support various claims. While this publication contains health information, it does not aim to provide advice or replace the advice of mental health professionals such as psychologists, psychiatrists, counselors, therapists, or health coaches, nor does it replace the insights of business coaches, career coaches, business advisors, financial advisors, or any other relevant industry professionals. Additionally, although the author is a licensed medical professional, this book does not offer medical advice, nor does it seek to replace or enhance the guidance readers and other users may receive from their qualified medical professionals. To that end, the content provided in this book is for informational purposes only. Should questions or the need for consultation of any sort arise, please seek the help of a qualified medical or business professional. The ultimate choice to make any decisions based on health or career falls upon guidance of the aforementioned professionals. As such, the author assumes no liability in connection with the use of this book.

The contents expressed in this book are the views and opinions of the author only and are based on a combination of the author's personal and professional experiences as well as research conducted by the author. Therefore, any anecdotes and personal experiences shared are personal recounts of the author's personal and professional life, and any semblance or parallels to other people's stories are purely coincidental.

CONTENTS

MUST READ:
A SELF-DIAGNOSIS OF
TELECOMMUTING PSYCHOSIS

WHAT you are about to read is not intended to slander or defame anyone or any company. It is merely an account of how telecommuting affected me psychologically and emotionally in ways I never could have imagined. I'll also share how I conquered these issues to regain control of my emotions—and my life. I am sharing my experiences to help others know they are not alone and the emotions they are experiencing are quite real. I've read many books and articles about telecommuting, but I have seen little attention devoted to the effects working in isolation has on one's psyche and well-being. I am writing this book to fill that void and provide hope, along with some strategies, as to how others might also thrive in a remote environment.

In this book, I'll share my journey into telecommuting, the unexpected toll it took on my mental health, and how I fought my way back to not only survive working from home but to *thrive* in a remote environment. As you read this book, you'll find my tips on how to optimize time management, increase productivity, set healthy work and professional boundaries, and preserve (and possibly improve) physical and emotional health. The best part is that you can achieve most of these tasks without leaving your home —unless you really want to.

When I became a full-time telecommuter, I noticed something about me wasn't quite right, but I couldn't put my finger on it. When I began telling friends and family members telecommuting was starting to make me crazy, they dismissed my statement as melodramatic. But that was also back in 2012—eight years before the COVID-19 pandemic spawned an unprecedented shift to remote work in nearly every industry like never before.

Although I have recovered, I am hearing more people complain about the toll telecommuting takes on one's mental health. Yet, sadly, the effects of telecommuting on a person's psyche remain severely understudied—even to this day.

I first started writing this book eight years ago but tabled it because I doubted anyone would want to read it. Now that COVID-19 has drawn attention to isolation and mental health like never before, I feel the call to write something I know can help so many. What you will read in the following pages is my unconventional introduction and journey into the world of telecommuting. I call my journey "unconventional" not because I am a pharmacist who works from home, but due to my approach in conquering the challenges of working in isolation. However, I recognize that for many people, the idea of a pharmacist telecommuting seems unconventional. Most envision a pharmacist as a medical professional who wears a white consultation jacket and works behind the counter. So, yeah, it probably sounds odd to think of a pharmacist as a professional who works from home.

I did not envision myself as a telecommuter, and my first two jobs that involved telecommuting were both pharmacy jobs, both occurring out of pure circumstance. Looking back, I believe that falling into telecommuting played a major role in my being overwhelmed by its challenges. Because I had never envisioned myself working from home, I found myself completely blindsided by the psychological side effects that come from teleworking. I thought my life would be easier, simpler. After all, what could be so difficult about missing a morning commute? I was in for a very rude awakening. I quickly learned I had underestimated how telecommuting would change my life and my career. I also became painfully aware of how being labeled as a remote worker carried stigmas that, in certain companies, could retard my career advancement.

Whether you are new to telecommuting or a seasoned pro, you know that telecommuting is not the walk in the park it appears to be. If you are reading this book, I would guess you are searching for reassurance that your strange feelings are not normal and you're not crazy. I'm here to tell you that you are not crazy. Not only that, but I can also assure you that any angst, distress, apprehension, doubt, depression, or other negative emotions you may be feeling are actual normal side effects as you adjust to your remote environment. And I am here to tell you that, over time, you will learn what works for you and how to manage your emotions. That said, for some, these intense emotions may always linger. Depending on how challenging these feelings become to manage, you might actually *choose* to stop teleworking and return to the office.

The COVID-19 pandemic has forever changed our world in many ways. For one thing, it created a safe space for people to have some very candid conversations about mental health, finally. While I am thrilled to see the destigmatization of mental health, the feelings are bittersweet. I suffered my challenges alone, and it took months to discover solutions and recuperate. For that reason, I wrote this book—so you'll already have an arsenal of solutions to battle the many complexities of telecommuting.

In the next pages, not only do I share my telecommuting journey, but I also offer key advice for surviving and thriving in a remote environment —with or without a pandemic.

In full transparency, I believe the recent explosion of studies about remote work and mental health is proof that I am on to something. As of October 10, 2020, searching for studies on solitary confinement and its effect on mental health in PubMed, a government database of scientific research, produced very few studies. When searching for "telecommuting," "teleworking," or "remote work" and "mental health" in the same database, I only discovered four articles. Three were related to the COVID-19 pandemic.

By January 19, 2022, there were forty-seven studies published about telecommuting and mental health in the previous year.[1] That's over ten times the number of studies published in 2020. The evidence is clear: researchers are also noticing the effects of teleworking on the psyche.

Not only that, but a quick Google search using the same keywords produced one study conducted back in 2003 with some interesting information. Although the article is behind a firewall, the excerpt states that the study compared the "psychological impact of teleworking to office-based work," and that the results indicated that remote workers wrestle with emotional stressors such as loneliness, worry, irritability, and guilt.[2] The researchers also observed that people who work from home experience "significantly more mental health symptoms of stress than office workers and slightly more physical health symptoms."

Perhaps previous studies evaluating the psychological effects of prisoners in solitary confinement might help highlight some of the harmful effects of teleworking. We now know that solitary confinement may produce negative effects on one's mental state. Some may become depressed, but left in isolation long enough, may eventually battle some form of mental illness. In late 2020, the International Symposium on Solitary Confinement, sponsored by Thomas Jefferson University, not only highlighted the mental effects of solitary confinement, but noted it can even shorten a person's lifespan.[3]

What does this have to do with working from home? A few years ago, I would have said, "Absolutely nothing." Now I would say the research on the psychological toxicities of solitary confinement offers yet more proof that isolation can wreak havoc on anyone's overall well-being.

While there is a growing body of studies that provide evidence regarding the effects of solitary confinement on mental health, as previously noted, the research exploring the effects of telecommuting on mental health appears painfully lacking.

Whether one lives with others also makes a difference. Having experienced both, I see that living alone amplifies the sensations of isolation. Teleworking while living with others can provide company, but it is challenging because roommates, family, significant others, or even a beloved pet may equate your physical presence with being socially available 24-7, even while working.

So, in addition to sharing my journey, I will share my hard-learned lessons and teach you how to thrive—not just survive—in a remote working environment. Not only does this entail time management and work strategy, but it also means setting clear boundaries. I discuss how to set boundaries for yourself—and for others—in Chapter 7 of this book. And unlike most books about telecommuting on the market, I will share studies and data on ways to preserve your physical and mental health. This includes how to take care of your body, including ways to prevent and eliminate back and neck pain and reduce eye strain. In other words, what I'm writing here is what other books are missing. These teleworking solutions will save you the time and energy of purchasing more books, researching answers, and suffering in silence—the way I did when I first started out.

Despite the challenges I faced adjusting to a remote work environment, I am grateful I stumbled into telecommuting. It has truly played a major role in defining what I want out of life. It helped me redirect my focus, establish my ideal path, set goals, and refine my values. The nature of telecommuting undoubtedly sped up the process and trajectory of my self-exploration.

As I said earlier, it was never my goal to be a telecommuter. Telecommuting sort of chose me. To be honest, I didn't fall into telecommuting. I *crashed* into it. My first opportunity to work from home came out of nowhere and in the unlikeliest of places. The experience taught me a lot about myself, the workplace, time management, people management, self-management, and life. These circumstances were a perfect storm of challenges that helped me evolve into my current self and redirect my energies to realize my true potential.

The concept of telecommuting is very broad and dynamic, and the formless nature of the remote workplace creates a great deal of uncertainty, vagueness, and ambiguity.

When I first began telecommuting, I talked to friends who worked from home and read numerous books and magazine articles on the topic. I gained some invaluable insights, but amidst all this information, I felt something was missing: no resources seemed to address the emotional and psychological aspects in depth. Most information seemed to focus on working efficiently and communicating effectively with coworkers and colleagues in a remote environment. Very little information—if any—addressed the psychological fallout one faces with the isolation of a remote environment. It was almost like taboo or some dark family secret *no one* dared talk about.

Naturally, I reached out to my support system—my family, friends, and colleagues—for help. However, because many of them had never worked from home at the time, nobody really understood my challenges. Frustrated, I felt completely alone and helpless. At one point, I even felt ashamed. After all, no one I'd met—even other telecommuters—admitted to any of these feelings. The absence of resources, support, and validation made me question my sanity and the validity of what I felt.

I cannot tell you how much I wish this book had existed then, if only to assure me I wasn't crazy. If nothing else, it would have helped me tremendously to realize I was not alone in my emotional turmoil and isolation.

So, I am writing this book not only as a form of therapy but also as a much-needed resource for those who are curious about or new to telecommuting and are wondering how to manage it. I want others to know their emotions are normal and the psychological effects of telecommuting are, indeed, real.

So, before I reveal the details of avoiding telecommuting psychosis and explain how to regain control of your life, I think it's important to share my backstory.

I don't claim to have all the answers, and this book is certainly not a replacement for professional medical advice. While individual opinions and results will vary, if sharing my truth, my journey, and my insights helps just one person, then I will have accomplished my mission.

Part I

The Hidden Impact of Telecommuting

Chapter 1

PHARMACY: AN ACCIDENTAL INTRODUCTION TO TELECOMMUTING

IF you would have asked me in 2009 where I thought I'd be working in 2010, 2020, or 2022, I might have said a pharmaceutical company. But I *never* would have said I would do it from home. I knew folks who were working from home back then. Yet, for some reason, I had *zero* desire to do so myself.

I had always envisioned myself working in an environment where I would interact with people I could actually see and touch. Perhaps that's what makes my career trajectory—and my journey—so interesting. I didn't find telecommuting; it found me.

Fast-forward to the spring semester of 2010. It was my last semester of pharmacy school, and a pharmaceutical company I'd been courting surprised me with a phone call.

"We have a position available and were wondering if you'd be interested," the recruiter said.

"Sure," I gushed before gathering any details about the position or its location.

"I know you're graduating in about six weeks, but we have an urgent need," the recruiter said with a detectable degree of hesitancy. "So... I was wondering if you'd be okay with working from home until you graduate... and then move to Chicago," she added quickly.

"Sure," I said, although I was completely unsure of how I would juggle a full-time job while finishing school. I remember hearing uncertainty in her voice and finding it odd. She seemed to doubt I would be interested in the job simply because it was remote. Because my eyes remained laser-focused on entering the pharmaceutical industry all throughout pharmacy school, I pushed her reluctant energy from my mind and allowed my brain to contemplate the logistics of working a full-time job while wrapping up the final weeks of pharmacy school. I envisioned myself strutting from the stage at graduation straight to an airport-bound taxi, ready to whisk me away to the Windy City before the ink on my degree dried.

As crazy as the story sounds, it is completely true. Also true is that I never heard from the recruiter—or the company—again. While waiting eagerly for the fateful call that never came obviously hurt my fragile, young pharmacist ego, the recruiter's ask planted a seed into my subconscious that would lie dormant until a year and a half later.

Anyway, at the time, I didn't see how working remotely fell into the plan of ascending to a high-ranking position. After all, I only knew about three people who had worked from home. And all three of them returned to an office setting in order to advance their careers. They told me working from home seemed to limit their opportunities for career advancement. However, this was also long before the COVID-19 pandemic, an important topic I'll address in a later chapter.

To be quite honest, my perceptions of a productive work environment and success were quite different. Pharmacy became my second career after a brief stint as a chemist. To date, I have yet to learn about any laboratory jobs that a person can legally handle at home. Historically, both chemistry and pharmacy careers required the employee to be at a physical office location. Nowadays, there are quite a few pharmacy jobs that are partially or completely remote—many of which existed before the pandemic.

However, the coronavirus has not only changed the number of people who work from home, but it has also caused a shift in the number of days per week people work from home. According to data collected by Statista.com, 47 percent of people living in the United States had never worked from home pre-COVID-19. That number jumped from 13 percent to 34 percent early in the pandemic. Eighteen percent of the people who participated in the survey said they worked from home less than one to two days per week. That number dropped 10 percent during the pandemic. Pre-COVID-19, only 17 percent of survey responders reported having telecommuted. That number more than doubled to 44 percent in April 2020 during the pandemic.[4]

The virus has taken an unprecedented toll on the global economy in ways previously unfathomable. While many people have lost their jobs, more companies employ workers remotely than ever before. And some corporations have made telework permanent. In May 2020, Jack Dorsey, the co-founder and former CEO of Twitter, famously announced that it was going completely remote.[5] About a week later, he granted Square employees that same option. After the social media platform mogul's declaration, numerous companies have followed suit. And companies that are requiring employees to return to the office have compromised with their subordinates, who have grown accustomed to and enjoy teleworking.

That said, my guess is remote work will become more mainstream—especially after corporations watch their bottom lines jump from reduced or minimal overhead.

Yet, notwithstanding the COVID-19 pandemic, technology would have likely continued tipping the scales in the direction of telecommuting. COVID-19 obviously played a role in this phenomenon, but one cannot ignore the financial benefit to brick-and-mortar companies. True, many companies have shut down in-office operations to help curtail the spread of the virus, but those companies managing to stay afloat no longer find it affordable or feasible to rent office spaces. With loyalty to the bottom line always front of mind for stakeholders, many companies are noticing that the elimination of on-site requirements also means the end of overhead, which is not only associated with office space but utilities, internet, maintaining compliance set by city ordinances, and other costs.

As technology keeps advancing at a lightning pace and many people seek to improve their work, skipping the daily commute is becoming more of a reality and less of a myth. In fact, between 80 and 90 percent of U.S. workers would like to work from home, according to a survey conducted by

Global Workplace Analytics in partnership with the United States Census Bureau.[6] In addition, the number of people employed as a telecommuter who aren't self-employed has grown a whopping 103 percent since 2005.[7]

Thanks to COVID-19, corporations are constantly exploring methods to increase or expand telecommuting options for their employees, and more employees are beginning to demand it. Technological advances and computer-based work make working from home easier than ever before.

My instincts also tell me that finance will most likely serve as a major driver in boosting the uptick in telecommuting—not just worker demands highlighted in "The Great American Walkout."[8] Companies are saving a great deal of money by allowing their employees to work from home. You don't need a PhD to see how this boosts the bottom line.

Working from home has some obvious benefits, many of which involve better work-life balance and improved quality of life—no commute, saving wear and tear on the car, more time with friends and family, less employee conflict, etc. As employee burnout remains a potential side effect of long hours in the office, more people are desiring the flexibility of a remote environment to improve their lives in the workplace and out of the office. But even with all its positive points, telecommuting still has some major drawbacks that often remain overlooked or understated.

For example, according to a study published in the *American Journal of Health Promotion* in 2016, how telecommuting affects one's health depends on the number of hours one works from home.[9] The study also suggests that the more hours one works from home, the more likely he or she is to have health concerns. Those working the most hours from home are more likely to be overweight, less likely to exercise, and more likely to abuse alcohol. But before accepting telecommuting as a sentence to a premature death, consider this: awareness is the first key to addressing the issue. It is entirely possible to work from home and live healthy—if not healthier.

After I started working from home full-time, my health improved. In fact, I lost weight and got in the best shape of my life. Despite the potential toll on my health and my initial anxiety about teleworking, I have truly come to enjoy working from home and believe it is the optimal work environment for me. As a writer, I need the peace and quiet that traditional and open-office spaces don't allow. For me, a home office provides a safe haven and the ideal work setting: a place devoid of the frequent interruptions, background chatter, and buzzing energy characteristic of most office environments. Over the years, I have come to find the groove that works for me and how to best manage my stress, work-life balance, and still live a full, healthy life outside of work. I'll share my tips in later chapters.

However, that's not to say that the beliefs I've adopted are the only way to tackle this issue. You'll find what works for you. In the same way yoga teaches us to take what we need and eliminate anything to our detriment, or that which complicates our lives, I encourage you to draw from this book, and my experiences, what serves you, and tailor it to fit your needs.

A few months after I began working as a pharmacist, my boss assigned me to a special project. I would continue traveling to various pharmacies to provide services, only this time, I would not be subbing for the pharmacists who were usually on duty. Instead, I would consult with patients one-on-one. I would schedule them for appointments, review all their medications, answer questions, and contact their doctors for additional help as needed.

The work was very challenging—as well as rewarding. But like most things worth having, the rewards came at some very high costs. I worked alone, so I had to wear multiple hats with no support. I already worked long hours in the pharmacy, and all the administration, research, and traveling lengthened my days while shortening my nights.

Sometimes, I would spend as many as five hours on the road. I was still lucky, though. At least with this gig, I was grateful I could sit down as soon as I got to the pharmacy. It also helped that my boss allowed me to work from either a store office or home office once or twice a week to handle administrative duties and phone calls. This unusual pharmacy job afforded me with my first experience of working from home—albeit a few days a week, tops.

I began looking forward to the days of working in my home office—for many reasons: I found myself much more productive without all the distractions and interruptions normally occurring in the pharmacy. Also, as an introvert, I needn't create meaningless small talk so others wouldn't think I was unapproachable or aloof.

Let me be clear: this was 2010 and 2011, so there was no pandemic, nor did I ask my boss to work from home. My teleworking environment erupted from a simple business need: the company did not have an office space at any of its stores or pharmacies where I could sit, make phone calls, handle paperwork, or do research.

For those of you who are not aware, before the COVID-19 pandemic, telecommuting sometimes became a double-edged sword. Recruiters viewed remote roles as highly coveted positions, and even when I would apply for jobs that explicitly stated the positions were remote, recruiters would dangle the carrot in my face and state that those positions were only for "exceptional" candidates. Although I am not a legal expert, this practice doesn't sound fair or honest in a country whose government allegedly strives for equal opportunity and fair hiring practices. If the remote option was not available to every candidate, then why not state that fact in the job description? Being more transparent would also warrant explaining what constitutes an "exceptional" candidate.

In other words, regardless of whether I worked from home a few days a week or every single day, one thing had become very clear: with my remote work environment came backlash and envy in the workplace. I was the only remote employee in my first full-time telecommuting position.

As a traveling pharmacist, I worked from home one to two days a week to catch up on the paperwork I could not complete while traveling to pharmacies within my region. On the days I'd set foot in a pharmacy, some of my colleagues seemed less than thrilled to see me. And to be honest, I cannot say I blame them. Even when I visited their pharmacies, I was usually meeting with patients individually, which meant I could do things considered both mythical and luxurious to many pharmacists who work in community settings: sit down and pee. Imagine standing on your feet all day, mainly in one spot, when your colleague comes waltzing in the office wearing pumps and touting a briefcase and the liberty to use the restroom whenever nature called. I might have hated myself, too.

My next pharmacist gig was fully remote—and I telecommuted by accident. I say "by accident" because the job was never intended to be remote —nor did I attempt to negotiate to use a home office. In fact, when I applied for the role, I understood two important things: First, I would have to become licensed to practice pharmacy in New Jersey and possibly New York. Second, I would also have to move to New York City if offered the job. However, both requirements changed during my interview with one executive. When he learned I had worked from home as a community pharmacist, he actually pitched to me the idea of working from home. His rationale?

"We need someone with experience in this area who can hit the ground running," he said. "Would you be comfortable working from home?"

Good thing it was a phone interview, so I could conceal my glee.

"I might be open to it," I said, trying to sound cool and unaffected. As soon as I hung up the phone, I squealed with delight.

After spending a year and a half ripping up and down narrow, two-lane roads with poor phone signal throughout rural communities in East Texas, I was tired of driving. While I truly loved working with my patients and found it very rewarding, my growing fatigue made it increasingly more difficult to serve them with the same level of energy and enthusiasm. The combination of the long hours on the road and at work had drained me in less than two years' time. I was burned out and ready for a change.

The new job spared the time and stress of long commutes. I also sensed the job wasn't something I would do forever. To be honest, the position itself didn't really excite me. I saw no growth potential, as it was very similar to what I was doing as a traveling pharmacist—without the road time. To be honest, I viewed it as a transition role that would allow me to maintain a steady income flow while recovering from burnout at my old job. I didn't see myself staying in the position for more than three months, but I still felt an overwhelming sense of relief and joy at the thought of fewer hours translating to better work-life balance.

Unfortunately, my excitement over this new direction quickly faded and transformed into self-doubt and fear after learning my family and friends did not share my enthusiasm. They all expressed similar concerns that I was throwing my life—and career—away. After all, I had worked so long and hard in school—and later in my job—to grow my career. And now, I was throwing it all away for an eight-to-five—at home?

"You'll ruin your chances for advancement," they told me. "Out of sight, out of mind." Translation: Accepting a remote position means you'll fade into obscurity.

"Why would you take a pay cut to work from home?" some said. "You're going backwards instead of forward." Translation: You're sabotaging your career!

"It sounds like you just need a vacation," others said. "After you take a break, you'll be ready to get back on the horse." Translation: Keep your current job because it pays more—even if you have no quality of life.

The list of negative feedback goes on—and on… and on….

The deluge of comments hit me so hard they were causing self-doubt and negative self-talk. But the fact of the matter is, I knew myself—and my body—well enough to know I had reached the point of no return, and I had a level of weariness no vacation or cup of coffee could ever remedy. I could not go back to spending hours on the road, nor could I stand on my feet for hours at a time.

Distancing myself from loved ones was not an easy choice, but I had reached a point where I did not need outside distractions to derail from making the best choice for me. That moment helped me to define who I am, what I want out of life, and how to create the best environment to be my best self.

With my priorities newly redefined, I traded in my consultation jacket and stilettos for yoga pants and flowy, moisture-wicking tops. Instead of spending an hour on the road to get to work, my morning commute entailed walking from my bedroom—or yoga mat—to my home office.

I guess you could say I was exploring how I defined myself and what made me Frieda.

Chapter 2

What Made My First Fully Remote Job More Brutal than Most (And Why I Can Talk about It Now)

M Y new home-based job with the New Jersey firm came with a pay cut. But the way I saw it, the quality of life was a priceless pay raise in exchange for zero commute time and major pain relief. Exhausted from my previous job, I officially retired my road warrior hat and haven't looked back since.

If I had a bad hair day or couldn't find a pair of matching socks, who would be there to notice or judge me? I wouldn't have to put on a brave face to mask my insecurities—or my discomfort. Since I had been working from home one to two days a week in my old job, working remotely would be a seamless transition, right?

Wrong. Looking back, I knew the interviewer had probably worked from home in a mostly remote role, at some point, by what he revealed in his question:

"Given that you have already had some telecommuting experience, I was wondering if you'd be comfortable working from home."

He did not ask me if I *wanted* to work from home. He asked me if I would be *okay* working from home. Huge difference. I didn't catch the hint at the moment, but I would later come to replay that conversation in my mind many times as the months flew by.

Asking me if I were comfortable working in a remote environment sort of implies challenges. However, I was so tired—and grateful for a job that provided new options—I couldn't see the forest for the trees.

The company also noted the role would require some on-site travel, so I assumed the lifestyle would pattern what I had experienced working in community pharmacy before (minus the longer hours and the long commutes, of course). Since it was an office job, I felt the "field days" would be easy to manage.

It was like the universe had answered my prayers. I couldn't believe my luck. But I would soon realize I was in for a very rude awakening: what seemed like a blessing would eventually turn into my biggest nightmare yet. The job that was supposed to restore my work-life balance would ultimately evolve into the exact opposite. Before it was all over, my physical, mental, and emotional health would take a severe beating in ways I never could have fathomed.

'How is that possible for a work-from-home job? How could you possibly feel depressed or experience physical health problems?' you might ask—especially if you're new to teleworking. Some of you seasoned telecommuters might not quite connect the dots here either, depending on the nature of your work and the degree of flexibility that comes with it. The problem is that not every work-from-home job has the same degree of scheduling flexibility. If you still don't follow, keep reading. You'll soon understand.

I had signed on the dotted line with the promise of work-life balance. I eagerly welcomed the idea of not standing on my feet all day and taking potty breaks whenever needed. You might laugh at that last item, but those of you who have ever worked in a pharmacy know *exactly* what I'm talking about.

Also, recall that, at the time I accepted the offer, I was told the job would not be 100 percent remote. Initially, I was expected to make periodic on-site visits—not only to meet the team, but to help with training. After all, when I was hired, I was the only pharmacist on board with experience in that particular area, so the idea that this promise would fall by the wayside never entered my mind. After life on the road most business days of the month, a trip for a few days every month or every few months sounded like the perfect balance: I could reconnect after being disconnected, and then return home to refocus and recharge.

But as time went on and days stretched into weeks, months went by without my making a single on-site visit. Yet the promises continued. As the only telecommuter in my department (aside from my boss), I felt isolated. The isolation grew during the times when I should have felt most connected and engaged with my coworkers—department meetings. Inside jokes and buddy banter between my colleagues often sifted into the meeting's discussions. But because I had never seen or met these people, I didn't feel comfortable chiming in. I felt alone and completely left out. Other times, I felt downright out of place, wondering if I would ever have an opportunity to build a relationship with my colleagues.

And the nature of my work intensified my isolation. Unlike my friends and colleagues who held remote positions at the time, I didn't have the luxury of packing up my laptop and heading off to a coffee shop or joining a co-working group. I also did not have the flexibility to take off a few hours in the day and make up the time later because I was involved in patient care. In other words, from 8:00 a.m. to 5:00 p.m., my entire workday was scheduled from start to finish. I had to complete two patient consultations every hour—and meetings often occurred on top of that.

Not only that, but my role lacked the location flexibility I'd previously heard about with telecommuting roles. Since my work involved handling health information and talking to patients on the phone regarding confidential matters, I couldn't take my laptop to the park or swing by Starbucks for an afternoon. Security and patient confidentiality were major priorities. And that meant much of the flexibility most telecommuters I knew enjoyed was not an option for me. That also meant renting a shared office space was out, too. In other words, I had to wait until after five o'clock to have meaningful social interactions. Sometimes, by the time I finished my workday, I was so starved for human contact those encounters could not quench my thirst.

Allow me to provide further context around how scheduling and location stringency affect my mental state as a person new to a fully remote role. Because each consultation was scheduled every fifteen to twenty minutes, I could not set my schedule—an autonomous privilege I instantly missed from my previous partially remote role.

The worst part was that nobody seemed to understand my frustrations. Most friends and family would describe me as never having a loss for words. Yet, in this case, I might as well have been mute. It didn't matter how I tried to explain my challenges. My words somehow failed to articulate my strife. Nobody understood my frustrations, and most people—even those who knew me best—trivialized them.

For example, when I vented to family and friends—people who knew me best—their responses shocked me.

"You work from home! What do you have to complain about?"

"You don't have to spend time getting ready and driving to work every day. Must be nice."

"You can set your own schedule as long as everything gets done."

"What are you griping about? You get to sleep and watch TV all day in your pajamas!"

When I met new people, their reactions to my remote work were equally frustrating. It always started with, "Oh wow! You have the dream job!"

"Why would you *ever* want to quit your job?"

Do any of these comments sound familiar?

What I found most amazing was that those who instantly assumed I was living my best life had never worked from home. They couldn't comprehend that not all telecommuting jobs were ideal. When I complained of lacking social interaction, even my own father said that after spending all day talking to patients on the phone, I should be tired of talking.

"But it's not the same, Daddy," I'd say, painfully aware that my comments had fallen on deaf ears. "Those conversations are work-related and nothing like chatting with friends and family."

As strange as it may sound, I actually looked forward to weekly conference calls at work because it gave me an opportunity to engage with all my coworkers in real time. It was the only time I felt "seen" or part of the team—even though all these meetings occurred by phone. My company was a startup that lacked the infrastructure to support videoconferencing in the pre-COVID-19 era of 2012.

So when those meetings happened, I actually enjoyed listening to my coworkers' voices. As crazy as it sounds, sometimes I'd close my eyes and try to imagine what my colleagues looked like, how they dressed, and other details, even down to the perfume or cologne they wore. Yup. I was truly that lonely—and I'm an introvert and often a loner! I know now I was coping with unexpected fallout of social isolation, loneliness, and perhaps depression. At the time, however, it was unfathomable for me to mention these issues to anyone. Again, the fallout of the COVID-19 pandemic has created a safe space to talk about these problems.

I cannot speak for how other telecommuters who stumbled into remote work in a similar environment adapted. In my case, by using imagination to simulate interaction with coworkers I'd never met, I had developed a coping mechanism. It was a feigned attempt to compensate for the absence of meaningful human contact. But of course, the sensory "experience" always expired at the end of the phone call. And I was left alone in a room.

The remaining thirty plus hours of the week, I was left alone in my thoughts and with my patients. I loved it—at first. Then I came to dread it worse than the early Monday morning meetings that occurred every week without fail. I presume my coworkers attended those meetings with little thought beyond our new deliverables and realignment. But for me, they were a recurring reminder I was missing out on the comradery and work relationships that appeared to brighten their days. Somehow, I had become a lonely ghost haunting the team from 1,000 miles away. Like a ghost, I was invisible—only I couldn't truly haunt anybody because nobody knew I was there.

Having limited one-on-one interactions with my colleagues at work brought me more misery. In fact, the only connections I had with my colleagues occurred via email and phone. The fact that nobody seemed to understand how alone I felt and why I was reaching out made me feel powerless and invisible.

One of my coworkers eventually sensed the isolation I was feeling without me saying a word. He began calling me every one to two days or so to strike up conversations. At first, it caught me off-guard. I questioned why he would care enough to reach out—especially when I felt invisible to the entire company and no one else seemed to care.

After a while, I let go of my inhibitions and allowed myself to welcome and appreciate the human interaction I craved. It was refreshing to have normal conversations with people at work that were not serious or intense, unlike my patient consultations.

As well-intending as my colleague might have been, his efforts could only do so much as the demands of the job changed. Now the increasing workload only enhanced my feelings of loneliness and isolation. As I jumped from call to call, I felt some of the robotic nature of my former position returning. I was crunching numbers all day. But this time, I wasn't being graded on the number of prescriptions I filled or patients I scheduled for one-on-one consultations. Instead, I was being graded on the number of patients I reached on the phone each day, and no matter how hard I tried, it seemed like my best was never good enough.

My calls were recorded (for quality purposes, of course), and as the department's only remote employee, I felt as if my every move was under intense scrutiny. Because nobody thought I was working, I developed an extreme sense of paranoia. I felt I had to work harder to prove that I was contributing to the team. So, I did. I stayed later—after my colleagues had already left for the day or the weekend. When I had no technical issues, I made sure that my numbers were higher than everyone else's. In general, I would like to think I am not a competitive person. This situation is no exception. I wasn't competing. I was proving that I was indeed working and not just lying on the couch in my pj's.

After all, friends and family, who had never telecommuted, thought I was living the life of luxury—and they knew me! So, why would the coworkers and boss I had never met think otherwise?

In addition to the angst about being considered lazy, other psychological torture began to set in. While I didn't have to spend hours on the road, I still suffered because I was left alone with my thoughts and my work. I didn't have the liberty of blowing off some steam with my work spouse or breaking up the monotony with the latest water cooler gossip.

I was my only coworker, sitting in a home office with a lonely window view of a quiet forest that kissed my backyard. I couldn't play music during the day because I was constantly on the phone. I rarely had time for breaks.

For the first time in my life, I felt completely isolated and alone. I didn't have anybody to talk to who understood my troubles. This only added to my grief. At one point, I began thinking I was losing my mind.

As the weeks dragged by, I lost the motivation to put forth the extra effort interacting with the outside world. With my social circle dwindling and my waning efforts to meet new people now falling through the cracks, I became even more depressed. And since no one seemed to understand my frustrations, the situation only brought on apathy and self-doubt. Maybe they were right. Perhaps I was complaining about nothing, and it was all in my head. Maybe I was losing my mind. And if I were sane, were my feelings even justified? After all, I no longer had to spend hours on the road and entertain workplace drama. Was it possible that spending nearly forty hours a week alone caused me to imagine things and exaggerate my situation?

To sum it up, my first fully remote gig was more brutal because I never expected to be fully remote in the first place. So, nothing could have prepared me for the psychological consequences of slipping through the administrative cracks of a company post-acquisition. And unlike the millions of people who were thrown into telecommuting overnight because of the COVID-19 pandemic, I had no colleagues in my department or in my regular network who truly understood.

I had to go it alone. There was no support system, and the company had limited technological resources to make it easier to connect with my colleagues or seek additional information. Having no instruction manual also did not help. Essentially, I found myself short on resources.

So, now that COVID-19 has created a safer space to talk about mental health, I am here to admit something very painful: I started to lose it—and the scariest part was that I saw my mental health decaying right before my nearsighted eyes.

Chapter 3

NINE MAJOR MYTHS ABOUT TELECOMMUTING

PLEASE don't take this the wrong way, but after a decade of telecommuting, I believe some people who have never worked from home may have a little trouble understanding how it works and severely underestimate its challenges. As I stated earlier, some skeptics perceive telecommuting as a blowoff job, envisioning people wearing their pajamas while streaming Netflix all day.

Chances are, if you're reading this book, you are probably a telecommuter, and your perception is likely quite different. If you have never worked from home, you might find yourself baffled by the concept that working from home can be stressful.

'How can telecommuting be stressful?' you might ask. After all, you get to sleep later and have more time to exercise and spend with family because you don't have to get dressed up and fight traffic during the morning commute and the five o'clock rush hour every day. Unless you live with other people, you technically have no real incentive to change your clothes —after all, it's not like your boss can smell you during a Zoom call. Some people may assume that working from home automatically means you can stay at home and watch television all day because you don't really have to work. Others might think that having a home offices automatically means you get to avoid all the workplace drama.'

And I understand why things may seem that way because I made many of the same assumptions—before I set up a home office.

In reality, every job has its challenges—no matter where or what it is. And as a telecommuter, if you plan to grow your career, you may face some challenges when seeking to make a career change.

I can't tell you how many job interviewers actually discounted my ability to work in an office with an address that didn't match my residential address. It was as if my current job erased my track record of in-office positions. In each case, I had to remind the interviewer I had worked in office settings before—as well as in corporate America. It doesn't get more "office environment" than that. I also had to educate one hiring manager on the concept that, as a telecommuter, you have a home office. In the most extreme cases, I actually had to explain that my home office was a separate room in the house with a computer, printer, and office furniture to help them "get it."

I'd also point out that, with autonomy comes greater responsibility and accountability. After all, if I weren't meeting deadlines or performing in my remote environment, that would come at a greater cost as a telecommuter than if the same thing were to occur in office: I might lose my boss' trust and have to relinquish the privilege of working remotely. Even worse, I might actually lose my job, whereas an in-house position might come with a disciplinary write-up or auditing.

One hiring manager actually complimented me on my ability to make eye contact. "After all these months of working in a home office, I didn't expect you to look me in the eye," the interviewer said, clearly stunned by my delivery. "But not only did you look in me in the eye, you've maintained eye contact for the entire interview."

I know she meant it as a compliment, but I have to admit that her statement took me aback. I was a telecommuter—not a hardened criminal trying to conceal a crime.

I smiled politely and then responded. "As a telecommuter, I tend to savor in-person interactions because they don't happen very often. I really appreciate having this conversation with you. Sometimes, I really miss the human interactions, and that's part of the reason this job interests me."

So, without further ado, I've outlined what I have found to be the nine biggest myths about working from home.

Myth #1: You work less than everyone else—if you work at all

It always amazes me how many people think telecommuters spend their days twiddling their thumbs glued to the television because they don't have to work. But the fact of the matter is the opposite holds true. You may work *harder* as a telecommuter than you did when you held an office position. Apparently, the pandemic has amplified this fact.

According to a *New York Times* article published in June 2021, some bosses may expect their employees to work longer hours because they are at home.[10] Anecdotally, I can report that some of my colleagues and friends who became first-time teleworkers during the pandemic complained that their bosses started giving them more work because they were at home.

Personally, I find this discouraging. While telecommuting may require a bit of an adjustment initially and isn't necessarily for everyone, it can actually increase productivity when done efficiently. For example, in my first fully remote job, I was often the top performer in my department.

So, if you are naturally driven and work well independently, you may find yourself much more productive and efficient as a telecommuter. After all, you won't need time to adjust and settle in after your commute to the office, and there may be fewer distractions. However, other responsibilities, such as homeschooling children, playing parent to furry babies, and taking care of elderly people, might throw a monkey wrench into the equation.

For example, maybe the phone is not ringing off the hook because you are no longer on-site to troubleshoot something requiring in-person interaction. And now, the office-gossip cheerleader no longer stops by your desk to collect intel on some fresh scandal to circulate around the office.

These are just a few examples, but some productivity drivers and disruptors also depend on your management. For example, if your boss is a micromanager, you may feel compelled to work harder, demonstrate your value, and show you are indeed working. This is no different from what you would experience if you were working in-house. If your coworkers are not remote, you may experience backlash and added pressure to produce or demonstrate value. I speak from experience.

Nowadays, since the COVID-19 pandemic, office disruptions that don't involve a spouse, child, or pet seem to have crept into the home office, too —thanks largely to technology. Zoom and Microsoft Teams calls are at an all-time high. Even though I am now a consultant, I will say that I have seen an exponential uptick in video calls my clients schedule. Many conversations that were once achieved conveniently and efficiently via email have now become scheduled video calls.

That said, I have realized some people schedule video calls because they are new to telecommuting and miss tangible human interactions. Yes, it can be an adjustment for everyone, but remember, the discomfort others are experiencing is not your responsibility if you are not their manager. You can work efficiently and productively without all the extra meetings —unless you would rather have them, too. I am not suggesting you skip work meetings. However, if you don't want to turn an eight-hour workday into a twelve-hour marathon, I urge you to consider devising a strategy that allows you to be present and communicative without adding more hours to your workday.

When I stepped into a contract role that required a full-time commitment in mid-2020, I quickly realized I needed to devise a strategy to improve my productivity and curtail the excessive meetings. For larger meetings, I would show my face and interact early to establish my presence, and then switch off my camera to multi-task. Sometimes, I had no choice but to grin and bear it. But as I familiarized myself with my work and the meetings kept piling up, I asked my client to review and prioritize meetings. I presented the issue as a concern of reduced productivity and proposed the client prioritize the meetings I attend while removing those that added little value to my work.

As for the meetings that proved inevitable, I collected and provided as much information as possible before the meetings, hoping to reduce camera time. Doing so allowed me to manage meetings and present the issues I could not solve alone or that were better explained by sharing my desktop. Not only did the client appreciate my preparation, but I often managed to cut thirty- and sixty-minute meetings in half.

Even if you enjoy video calls, "Zoom fatigue" is a real thing and may push you to burnout from your work environment. And to prove I'm not complaining, here's the data to back this up.

According to an article published by the Pew Research Center, many people in certain professions who telecommute say the amount of time they spend on video calls wears them out.[11] Sadly, that accounts for nearly half the people working in the educational industry (44 percent), 33 percent of those in scientific and professional services, 29 percent of those working in accounting and real estate, and 25 percent of those working in information and technology. Still, many people working in each of these industries confess online engagement is an acceptable alternative when face-to-face interactions are not possible.

What you will probably discover—if you haven't already—is that setting boundaries becomes extremely important to protect your sanity as much as it does your work-life balance in the world of teleworking. I discuss boundaries in a later chapter.

So, how might you find yourself working harder without extra distractions disrupting your concentration? There are several reasons this might happen. I will offer my own personal experience for starters. When I initially began working from home as a community pharmacist one to two days a week, some of my colleagues seemed a bit frustrated and would try to find assignments for me to complete in addition to the meetings I had scheduled, the paperwork I had to complete and file, and reports I had to create for upper management. Because I was new to the workforce, I struggled with how to manage this conundrum. Declining or delegating might indicate that I was not a team player and therefore affect my performance review and raise. However, I was human and already overloaded with projects; I was a one-woman show who played the clinician, the administrator, the receptionist, and the advocate.

Ultimately, I made a choice I would not make today. I pitched in even if it meant I worked more hours or had to put other tasks on the back burner.

And do you think they acknowledged my extra efforts in my performance review? Absolutely not. As you can imagine, I found the snub discouraging. The longer I stayed with the company, the more my resentment grew.

Anecdotally, I have heard people thrown into telecommuting during the COVID-19 pandemic say they are now given more work to complete. I don't understand the rationale myself, but I suspect employers see the lack of commute as an opportunity for more work to consume your newly spare time.

Again, while I haven't experienced this issue myself, trying to gain clarity and maintain a good line of communication with your supervisor about realistic goals seems important.

Myth #2: You are living *the life*.

I won't lie. Once I started working from home just a day or two a week, I couldn't see myself going back into an office every single day. I immediately enjoyed the escape from the intense office bustle and the break from the hour-long, one-way commute. However, part of my relief also came because a remote environment complements my personality. I am a highly sensitive person, and the bustle of the in-house positions often overwhelms me and leaves me exhausted.

Personally, I find I am more productive—not to mention happier—in a remote involvement. I have trouble staying focused and on task with the constant stimulation that comes when working in-house. Not only am I more productive when I have minimal distractions, but my work tends to be of higher quality, too. I think it also helps that I am a natural introvert who enjoys working independently. While I don't mind teamwork, I do prefer to work alone rather than in a group because I think—and perform —better this way.

But this is my personality. Many people I know do not work well in the environment I just described. However, despite my admitted introversion and love of independence and self-management, I do still enjoy social interactions. It took me working from home to realize just how much even the smallest social encounters mattered. Many of my colleagues who telecommute agree.

When I first began working remotely, I realized how much I missed socializing. And it's not just shooting the breeze with an "office spouse" or Enchilada Thursdays with favorite coworkers. Sometimes, it's the simplest encounters that take their toll. For example, maybe you talk shop with the manager at the neighborhood cleaners each week when dropping off your clothes. Or maybe you enjoy trading creative coffee recipes at the Starbucks on the same street as your office. You might even find yourself longing for brief-yet-regular social interaction chatter with regular customers while waiting in line at your favorite coffee shop. It can be lonely at first, but recognizing the void is the first step to overcoming the challenges and warding off depression or a melt-down.

Not everyone works well in this environment. And even if you think you might, sometimes it's hard to tell until you find yourself in the remote world. As an introvert who landed remote roles unexpectedly, I had to learn this the hard way.

Initially, I was okay working from home a couple of days after spending four or five hours a day on the road because I still felt connected and like I was part of a team. But as I began spending more time at home, I felt a disconnect when I'd head back into a pharmacy. Sometimes, it would be as simple as missing a logistics update or a new policy implementation. Other times, it was the little things that don't necessarily affect the logistics of the job but simply add character to the workplace: maybe a co-worker got engaged, or an encounter with a colorful patient added some pizazz to the workplace that day. Then one day, hearing an inside joke makes you realize you are now on the outside looking in—or at least that's how I felt. As a full-time telecommuter, I would hear the comradery and could feel the team synergy practically radiating from the phone during our team meetings. While I enjoyed hearing my coworkers' warm interactions with each other, as the weeks dragged on, witnessing their increasing closeness made me feel more distant and isolated.

I felt like an orphan, and because more than a year would pass before any of my teammates would work from home, nobody understood the loneliness I felt.

Myth #3: All telecommuting jobs allow you to set your schedule.

I have experienced the extremes of both scheduling situations in my career: setting my own schedule and having every single minute of my workday predetermined for me. My first telecommuting job actually *required* me to set my own schedule because I needed to define the days I would fill prescriptions in pharmacies; but I also needed to schedule appointments with physicians, patients, corporate managers, and potential business partners.

My second job took out all the guesswork that comes with coordinating a schedule because the groundwork had already been established. The program was already in place, and other staff members handled the administrative duties so we pharmacists could focus exclusively on our interactions with the patients. In fact, everything was so established that my entire workday consisted of back-to-back patient consultations and company meetings. Much like the stories you hear about community pharmacy, I almost needed to schedule my restroom breaks.

With that said, my experiences aren't the rules or the exceptions. There are many variations in telecommuting. The role of the remote worker is continuing to evolve and remains as dynamic as today's workplace. Obviously, the COVID-19 pandemic has only added to that.

Myth #4: All telecommuting jobs are 100 percent home-based.

This may sound like an oxymoron, but believe it or not, many telecommuting jobs require significant amounts of travel. Oftentimes, the positions require travel three to four days a week with work out of the home office on the remaining business days.

As you have probably already noticed, my first telecommuting job fell into this category. When I first began telecommuting in community pharmacy, I split my time between store offices and my home office for several months. After that, I was on the road four to five days a week and averaged only one or two days in the home office over a two-week period. There are a variety of these roles labeled as telecommuting positions. A classic example is an account executive position.

I have encountered this label with many jobs posted as "remote" or "home office" positions. Some roles, while listed as "remote," will include the percentage of travel expected in the job description. Others require a little detective work. If you are seeking a job that involves more telecommuting than travel, you'll quickly learn to read between the lines and ask the interviewer the right questions.

Myth #5: All telecommuting jobs allow you to work—and live—wherever you want.

My first telecommuting job required me to live within certain geographic proximity to the company headquarters and their surrounding stores. Given the fact that each office day required a significant amount of road travel to areas that were still a few hours away from the nearest airport, being local was essential. Air travel, transportation, car escort services, trains, and other forms of public transportation were not options.

On that same note, some sales jobs are listed as "remote," but they may also require the employees to live close to a metropolitan area with easy airport access.

On the opposite end of the spectrum, my second remote job was the total package: I could live wherever I wanted. However, the geographic flexibility came with two major drawbacks. First, I could not set my own hours. I had to work a standard eight-to-five schedule every single day (and sometimes extended hours to ensure our team met its quota). Second, because my work required patient consultations every fifteen to thirty minutes throughout my entire workday, flexibility was not an option. I also had to remain on-hand for spontaneous meetings and internal-phone calls.

Translation: I couldn't take a few hours to run to a doctor's appointment or pick up my nieces from school and then return home to wrap up my workday in the evening. It also stunted my career development. Dropping in on afternoon or early evening networking events in Houston traffic was out of the question. Imagine trying to interview for other jobs on that schedule. And at the time, most employers did not seem sympathetic to my situation—even when the company suspended the pharmacy team's vacation leave because they needed us to complete more cases.

The lack of understanding of my schedule affected personal activities, too. To illustrate this challenge, at one point, I was taking private Pilates classes two to three times a week. The studio was about forty minutes away from my home. I eventually stopped going because my instructor refused to understand why I could never make daytime appointments the way her other telecommuting clients did. I grew tired of explaining myself.

Today, as a consultant myself, I have developed a new respect for entrepreneurs who set their own schedules. Clients tell me when they want projects completed all the time. I may not necessarily care about the due date, but as a consultant, I recognize my clients are paying me for my services, not my opinions. If I want to eat, and I want their business and referrals, I have to be flexible. Otherwise, I'll have to find clients who cater to my exact schedule and needs or change my business model altogether.

As I mentioned in a previous chapter, the other major drawback to my job was the sensitive nature of my work, requiring me to remain home the entire time. Because I was handling confidential health information, I had to take special care to secure my laptop and any work-related documents. I also had to ensure that my calls remained confidential. That meant those impromptu trips to my favorite coffee shop and dropping in on random join-ups with coworking groups were gone. More specifically, the confidential nature of my work prevented me from joining coworking groups, sitting at the library, or taking my laptop to the park on a beautiful sunny day. Because I was 100 percent remote, busy season felt more like house arrest than a long day at the office.

Instead, I replaced those privileges with a permanent home office setup. I converted an unused room in the house into a full office. Originally a patio, the converted room still had the originally sliding glass door, which concealed my conversations—and my office—from the rest of the house. While this "protected" environment increased my productivity by helping me focus, it also amplified my isolation from all human contact.

What made my situation more severe was the fact that I originally expected to travel with my job, so the intensity of isolation never entered my mind as a side effect. I believe that my situation would have been different if the company had not been acquired a few months after I was hired. I also believe that I likely would have had some travel and interaction had this not happened. After the acquisition, I sort of fell through the cracks. I kind of felt like the company's management team had forgotten about me. Let's just say that my invisibility gave new meaning to the phrase, "out of sight, out of mind."

I had no way of knowing that things would change or how they would evolve. Nor could have I anticipated the isolation. Once I realized my role might never involve travel, I took it upon myself to create a new destiny. I began seeking out volunteer opportunities as a way to meet new people and shift my focus to other people instead of myself. I also set up vacation rentals in cities I liked or wanted to visit.

Myth #6: You have zero problems or workplace drama

Telecommuting requires a higher level of skill most times because you have to become comfortable working with many unknowns, limited information, and unless you have a micromanager, limited guidance. Sometimes, that means you will face hurdles in clear or complete communication. You can also expect to have technological problems. Sometimes, it's because of the internet connection, so you may need to upgrade your internet to support massive file uploads and downloads and video calls. Or it's because the company sent you a computer on its last leg. Or perhaps you spend a day unable to work because you can't log into your company's secure network or connect to its virtual private network (VPN) because the company's security flags your internet service provider as "suspicious."

With more people now than ever working from home during the pandemic, the extent of technological challenges telecommuters face is becoming more widely known and accepted. However, there was a time when that was not always so.

I'll confess that I do not miss the dynamics of dealing with unique personalities in the workplace. That said, just because you work in a home office does not necessarily mean your work environment will be drama-free.

You can still have a micromanager boss. I hear horror stories from friends and former colleagues who say their bosses don't trust them to get their work done at home. To compensate for their absence in the office, some bosses and companies may require their employees to check-in via video in the new remote environment. I was fortunate my company lacked the technological infrastructure to support video calls. But it still didn't prevent me from falling victim to random pop-up meetings—or my supervisor calling the moment I stepped away to use the bathroom.

"I called (or sent you an instant message), Frieda, but you didn't respond. Where were you?"

Sound familiar?

Myth #7: Telecommuting is not a skill set

Again, I'm prefacing this myth with the assumptions I'd encountered as a new telecommuter. I'm not sure I quite follow the rationale behind thinking working from home requires less skill than sitting in an office with other people. If anything, it often requires a *higher* level of skill, in part for one of the reasons I'd mentioned in Myth #6: You may sometimes need to work with less information and fewer resources than what you might have taken for granted when you worked in-house.

For example, some companies might offer orientations and instructional manuals on how to find policies, use various website portals, and handle day-to-day tasks. However, sometimes the information is not always available, is hard to find, or outdated. In an office setting, you might have the liberty of asking a cube buddy to help sort out an issue. Sure, perhaps you could send him an instant message on a company platform (if available) or text him if you have his personal cell. But you may not get an immediate response the way tapping them on their shoulder or swinging by their desk might. And not having an answer can be a challenge when you need an immediate response.

Fortunately, today, many companies have a technological infrastructure allowing employees to interact with one other quickly and easily throughout the course of the day. However, only a short time ago, such was not the case. Surprisingly, the company for which I telecommuted full-time in 2013 lacked communication platforms, such as an instant messaging system or videoconferencing, to support frequent interactions.

A colleague who first telecommuted back in the 1990s told me that document-and file-sharing at her first remote job meant dropping a package in the mail! So, just be grateful for how far technology has come.

Myth #8: Everyone enjoys and wants to telecommute

Telecommuting taught me so much about myself, other people, and the world of work, perhaps in ways I might not have fathomed otherwise. It also taught me about my values and personality.

For instance, as I've noted, it's also important to recognize that not all personality types thrive in a home-based environment.

While I personally prefer to work remotely, over the years, I've met quite a few people who have worked from home but then decided to return to the office. One of these people was my "office spouse" from my first fully remote job.

When he and the rest of my pharmacy team began telecommuting, about fourteen months after I started, they also faced challenges. However, unlike me, they still had a team rapport for support—something I never truly experienced. Years later, when I bumped into my former "office spouse" at a conference, after we'd both moved on to different opportunities, he had a confession.

"I just couldn't stand working from home all the time and being alone," he said. "It was a good experience, but it's not for me."

The confessor was none other than the coworker who'd call and keep me company during my worst period of isolation from everyone else. He, like other people I knew, made a conscious choice to return to a traditional office setting. However, resuming in-person work may not always be an option for everyone. Regardless of whether you choose or need to telework, you can still have meaningful social interactions. You just might need to exert a little more effort to get started.

The good news is that many organizations have begun implementing various initiatives to help their employees manage their mental health and help them thrive in a remote environment—largely thanks to the COVID-19 pandemic.[12] According to research conducted by the Society for Human Resource Management, 67 percent of 550 U.S. employers who responded to a survey from March 12, 2021, to March 16, 2021, stated they were enacting strategies to support employees who were new to telecommuting. Some offer wellness programs, such as yoga and meditation services, which were already on the rise pre-pandemic. Now, those services, along with video check-ins and team-building activities, can help both telecommuting newbies and veterans feel supported and more engaged.

Myth #9: You are *always* available

When I became a full-time telecommuter, a fellow pharmacist who had entered the world of remote work long before I did, gave me some advice I have never forgotten. I use it every day—even now as a small business owner.

"Frieda, you need to set your boundaries right away," she told me in a very stern tone. "Because if you don't, they will abuse you."

And that's exactly what happened. Looking back, I remember the glowing red flag of a superior who kept pressing for a meeting *before* my official start date. True, I thought it was both ridiculous and unnecessary, but I also struggled with the idea of tarnishing my reputation before I had even started work. The last thing I wanted was to be labeled as "difficult."

However, I was also annoyed because I was also on vacation, trying to enjoy my last moments of freedom, and rejuvenate myself from the road warrior burnout I'd endured the month before. Yet, management seemed to have no regard for my vacation (yet another glowing red flag). So yes, I continued to receive emails and phone calls about this "necessary" meeting.

Finally, I acquiesced, and became instantly irritated after realizing the meeting was unpaid and had no actual sense of urgency. So then, why all the phone calls and emails? To be fair, I also attended a mandatory meeting with the director of pharmacy and a human resources representative before starting my job as a floating pharmacist. But they *paid* me for my time. I erroneously assumed the same would hold true here. This aggravation foreshadowed what was to come.

Originally, my workday was supposed to end at 5 p.m. CST, or 6 p.m. EST to coincide with the time zone in New Jersey. Yet, for whatever reason, I would receive phone calls at 4:59 p.m. CST right on the dot. And when I began having technical issues with equipment, the offshore team would call me on Saturdays to work on my computer. I later discovered my boss had instructed them to call on Saturday mornings—without consulting with me or giving notice. At first, I felt abused and powerless. My solution? I treated the after-hours disturbances as spam calls. I blocked the phone number from the IT help desk.

My manager insisted I make myself available after hours to resolve my computer issues. I pushed back. After all, did my colleagues who drove into the office also need to show up beyond core business hours for meetings and troubleshooting? So then, why did I—especially when I was the top performer on the days my computer didn't have a gremlin in it? And if my computer wasn't working during business hours, why did I have to carve out personal time for support when it was clearly not resolving my technical problems *during* the week?

"The weekends are my personal time," I told her, trying to suppress my urge to scream. "I travel during the weekends, and for security purposes, I do not bring my computer."

And actually, this was true. Plus, after they woke me up early one Saturday morning, I also learned to turn my cell phone off. I was one of those weirdos who had a landline (still do) as a backup, so people could reach me in case of an emergency. I was very grateful they did not have *that* number. Obviously, my boss did not appreciate my response, but once she realized I would not budge, she eventually left me alone. And the incident(s) never made its way into my performance review either.

At this point, you might think (1) that my boss was overbearing—something I will not dispute, and (2) that this is an unusual case. But unfortunately, this overreach happens to others, too, regardless of the industry. A friend who works in the oil and gas industry has been a hybrid in-house/remote worker for years. And on her telecommuting days, she never fails to get a phone call right when the day should come to a close.

Looking back, I believe if I had refused the meeting before my start date, it would have signaled clear boundaries to the company.

My advice: Be *very clear* on what a separation between work and personal life looks like. Establish those boundaries from day one. And as my story shows, it's still possible to re-establish boundaries after the fact. However, it's more challenging, as you've already set a precedent for what you will and will not tolerate.

Chapter 4

TELECOMMUTING PSYCHOSIS: THE SIDE EFFECT OF REMOTE WORK NOBODY—AND I MEAN NOBODY— WANTS TO TALK ABOUT

Now that I've set the stage for some of the many challenges you might face as a remote worker, let's discuss how these challenges may ultimately alter your state of mind into a form of insanity. I hinted at this issue when I mentioned the effects of isolation on mental health in the first chapter. As for the insanity part, I am qualified to examine it because I've been there—and back.

I call the psychological challenges people face "telecommuting psychosis." This name, used to describe the extreme toll telecommuting takes on one's health, hasn't been applied in teleworking books or research, but I think the name fits—especially when nobody believes or understands the severity of the problem.

Despite all the challenges many of us have faced in the pandemic's wake, perhaps one of the greatest blessings has been an increase in the number of remote workers, as well as a more positive reception to the hurdles we telecommuters face. More people are speaking out, and they understand the challenges because, even if they don't work from home, their partner or best friend does. After more than a decade of having worked in a variety of remote environments, I finally feel safe coming forward. Thankfully now, we have much more data to support my claims.

Depression

There are many reasons why telecommuting can be depressing. While it is nice to shorten your commute to the office, you may quickly find yourself entering the world of unknowns and anxiety. In many ways, the experience in my first fully remote position models some experiences first-time telecommuters began undergoing during COVID-19, when they transitioned unexpectedly from an office environment to a fully remote setting.

Being forced into this environment suddenly and unexpectedly, without ample time to prepare, can be challenging. While the data to exploring the impact of telecommuting during the COVID-19 is still unfolding, data from previous studies indicate that working from home can have some negative effects on your mental health.

One study shows that people who work from home less than eight hours a month did not experience as much depression as people who worked from home full-time.[13] However, the data doesn't draw a strong link between depression and working from home a greater number of hours.

Isolation and Loneliness

Although I have not talked to every telecommuter in America, I think it's safe to say I have experienced some of its extreme pitfalls. Because I became a fully remote employee unexpectedly in my second telecommuting role, I can empathetically relate to many of the psychological and structural challenges many of you may have experienced if you began telecommuting because of the COVID-19 pandemic.

The isolation and loneliness I suffered were my greatest struggles. And as it turns out, I'm not alone. Sixteen percent of remote workers stated loneliness as their prime challenge as a telecommuter, based on a report in 2021.[14] That number increased 3 percent from 2019, but the report does not explain why that's the case.

As I'd mentioned earlier, I had felt like an outsider when returning to the pharmacy after a day or two. However, those feelings were minor compared to what I experienced working in complete isolation five days a week. To be fair, a few issues probably made my situation a bit more extreme.

First, all my coworkers were working in an office. Their office was in a completely different state. Initially, I was in a small Texas town on the outskirts of Houston. They were in Hoboken, New Jersey—walking distance from some of the most spectacular views of the New York City skyline.

It also did not help that I had never seen or met any of them in person—including my boss. At that point, most of them didn't have much of a social media presence either, so I invented in my mind what they looked like. It's one thing to have conversations with someone, but enduring meetings with the same coworkers several times each week felt odd when I had absolutely no clue what to think of their silence and some of their comments. I eventually developed a keen sense of discernment that allowed me to read their voices and the silence, but initially, it was like talking to a room of ghosts. I felt haunted and tormented by not really knowing whether I should read between the lines or take everything at face value. To be fair, I could possibly attribute some of my confusion to cultural differences. After all, I grew up in the south, and most of my colleagues were from the East Coast. Southerners are famously indirect, but initially, I had a little trouble figuring out the nuances of East Coast directness versus hints. I had never been embedded in the culture. I had a lot to learn.

Perhaps my biggest lesson working from home came from my initial ill-founded expectation: I automatically assumed working from home every day would not differ much from teleworking a few days a week. Because I made that assumption, I was completely unprepared for the psychological adjustment. Everything I encountered felt like an ambush.

During our standing meetings every Monday morning at 7:30 CST, my coworkers would joke with each other in a way that demonstrated their comradery. Much like my pharmacy days, they would make inside jokes or pick up where they had left off on a group conversation from the previous week. Yet again, I felt left out, like the red-shirted football player seated on the sidelines watching everyone play in the game. I'm sure my coworkers

45

didn't intend to leave me out, but to listen to them laugh with each other week after week, when I shared neither the story nor their history, made me feel very alone. I knew I could never become part of the team.

Remember the coworker who realized I felt left out? Here's where he began calling to check in with me a few times a week. He would fill me in on some of the office changes and even began joking with me a little. Over time, I came to very much appreciate his reaching out and our working relationship. I now understand he felt sorry for me. I wanted no one's pity, but I am forever grateful that he cared—and he tried—to help me cope.

Inability to Unplug

According to a report published by Buffer.com, nearly one third of remote workers (27 percent) stated unplugging as their greatest problem—a 5 percent increase from 2019.[11]

When you sit at your computer all day, it's hard to turn it off—or resist the urge to check your email. The fact that your workplace also happens to be the place you live can make it extremely difficult to separate the two. I offer some solutions on how to remedy this issue and create a separation between home-based work and home life in Part 2 about thriving as a telecommuter.

Sometimes, the inability to unplug can be a circumstance of your working environment, but employee conflict and interpersonal differences can also be a major pain point, too.

As a remote worker, I was frustrated by coworkers and management who had the impression that (1) I was always at home and (2) they could call me whenever—even outside of working hours, including dreadfully early on Saturday mornings.

Lack of Stimulation

It's important to point out the numerous factors affecting one's experience in telecommuting. The list is long and variable, but can include the company size, resources, culture, nature of the job, direct management, senior management, and many more.

In my second telecommuting job, our company was new to the field. Since that time, I have learned many ways of working as a telecommuter, such as consulting for larger corporations with more established infrastructure to support telecommuting. In my second telecommuting role, I worked for a growing startup company that lacked the resources and capability to support an optimal remote-working environment.

When I was first hired, I was the only pharmacist on the team who had previous experience in medication therapy management. Even though I had only about a year of experience in the field, I was initially the "expert" on the team. Even so, I quickly felt as if my isolation stunted my professional growth. I was not growing as a clinician.

My fellow coworkers had the benefit of listening to each other's consultations as they were happening, so they could grow and learn from one another. I gained new insights from other pharmacists during the team reviews, where we would listen to three or four calls made by other pharmacists on the team, grade them for quality, and discuss key insights as a team. I found this activity highly valuable, but for me, it only occurred once in a blue moon. Meanwhile, my colleagues had some version of this experience all day, every day.

The other drawback came from a lack of interactions with senior management or those working in other areas of the company. Since I wasn't given the opportunity to observe how different departments worked together, my feelings of isolation increased. It also limited my ability to identify areas for improvement and understand key insights that contributed to the importance of the work I did.

Stagnated or Limited Networking Opportunities

As I mentioned earlier, the constraints of my work schedule eroded any potential flexibility that so many telecommuters often enjoy. I struggled to network and meet new people who lived in the Houston area, and I fared even worse at my job. As the sole telecommuter on my team, I lacked the emotional support of comradery in the workplace, as well as the visibility that often results in mentorship, promotions, and other forms of career advancement.

I'm convinced that my invisibility truly hurt my chances of advancing at my first fully telecommuting job. At one point, I attempted to use the weekly and pop-up meetings as an opportunity to share new ideas and demonstrate my value, but my suggestions often fell on deaf ears. I also noticed my dismissed ideas were well-received when presented by others who were visible. Perhaps the fact that I was the only remote employee in my department amplified my feelings of isolation, frustration, and career stagnation.

As it turns out, my suspicions were not ill-founded. According to an article published in *Human Resources Director* in 2013, almost 80 percent of executives participating in a survey reported allowing their employees to work remotely in many different industries.[15] Yet, more than half believe that teleworking could limit employees' opportunities for career advancement. Perhaps the pandemic has shifted the mindset somewhat, but to what extent remains to be seen.

When I became a full-time telecommuter, I quickly discovered the role in and of itself had limited opportunity for growth and development. Add that to the fact that I was growing restless with my current role, as I acquired no new skills beyond what I had brought to the table to accelerate my transition into new opportunities with other companies. I quickly realized my complete invisibility had tanked my chances of advancement. I also feared the inability to develop new skills might limit my career. At the time, it appeared to me that nobody really seemed to value telecommuting as a skill, so I doubted its value, too.

I was ready to make a change, but the networking hurdles I faced made it virtually impossible to establish meaningful new connections—within the company and elsewhere. Even so, I refused to let my working environment halt my career progression—at least not without a fight.

Three months after I was hired, the company was acquired by a larger corporation based in Atlanta. The acquisition amplified my isolation and ghostlike invisibility because my needs as the lone teleworker in my department took a back seat to all the logistics and growing pains associated with mergers and acquisitions. Nearly a year and a half after I started working for the company, I finally met my boss and coworkers—after they had laid off most of the staff in the New Jersey office. The vice president of the new company was also present, and I used the opportunity to acquaint myself with him. Given my lack of opportunity to network with coworkers, I thought I would feel him out a bit first before revealing my desires for advancement. I decided to have that discussion after some time had passed, but I wasn't quite sure when—or how—that would happen.

Luckily, that encore meeting happened sooner than later when the parent company sent me to its headquarters in Atlanta. A chance meeting with an experienced human resource professional who happened to be dining next to me at a restaurant in downtown Atlanta fired me up. The woman shared some wonderful insights on how to present my case as a win-win for the company and for me. The new company had already established offices near me in Dallas and Houston, and she suggested asking to make site visits could be the perfect avenue to get the ball rolling. At first, I hesitated, but the more she talked, the more my ambition grew.

Months of depression from isolation and job dissatisfaction had eroded my confidence and self-assurance, but by the time I'd finished eating, she had pumped me up to fancy myself as the Wonder Woman of Corporate America.

The very next day, I arrived at the corporate office with my head held high and an extra spring in my step that earned a few double-takes. I felt invincible—ready to take on the world and anything beyond. I confidently requested a one-on-one meeting with my VP (who was my boss' boss), which he graciously granted for later in the week.

I was so excited to have the conversation that I felt ready to explode. The days and hours leading to that moment couldn't pass fast enough, as I knew it would be a major turning point in my career. Yet, for all my good intentions, I could not have foreseen the events that took place—which definitely marked a pivot in my career, but not exactly how I had originally anticipated.

That fateful meeting occurred after lunch on a Thursday afternoon. I confidently strolled into the VP's office. After a short round of corporate banter, I presented my case to close the deal.

"I really appreciate you carving out time from your busy schedule to meet with me," I said. "I wanted to run something by you. As you know, I have been with the company for nearly a year and a half. When I don't have technological glitches, I'm usually the top performer on my team. I hope you'll take that as a sign of my dedication to the company, and so I was hoping I could be stretched a bit. Since you have some offices in Texas, perhaps I could do some site visits and get a sense of the work they do. Maybe I could contribute to their teams in the future."

Watching the smile on the Alabama native's face melt into a stern gaze prepared me for the upset to come. They were running the heat in the building that day, but I felt the November draft sweep over the room.

"Yes, Frieda, I've seen your numbers, and they are good," the suit said, sounding irritated. "But people who work in those offices, who are assigned to their roles, understand those are their jobs and nobody else's. You are assigned to your specific department to do a specific job."

His words stung like a toxic venom seeping into the skin from a fresh snakebite on a simmering summer day. His sudden negative energy both confused and startled me. I found his instant rejection equally puzzling. His reaction also confirmed something I felt I had to do: move on. Not one to hold my tongue, I allowed my frustration to overrule my decorum.

"Well, I appreciate your candor," I said, trying to maintain the evenness in my voice, hoping to conceal my anger. "You were the last person in the company I was going to ask." I felt I didn't have to tell him he was my last resort to try to improve my future with the company. Less than a month later, I submitted my resignation.

I share this dark and very painful moment in my career with you, not as a sob story, but to offer insights on how you might approach a discussion with decision makers in your company to increase your own visibility, move forward, and hopefully, up.

While management did not seem fond of my offers to take on additional projects or contribute to areas beyond my scope of work, that doesn't mean rejection will become part of your narrative. These conversations are challenging, but sometimes we remote workers need courage to pursue our ambition—even if we fail or encounter rejection in the process. Otherwise, those who might be helpful may never know your desires—and those opportunities you long for may never materialize. In other words, you might hear a "no" if you ask, but if you never advocate for yourself, you've automatically guaranteed yourself a "no."

While my situation was perhaps a bit dire, fortunately, the pandemic has caused a positive shift in the way people now network. While we might not have enjoyed as many in-person networking events, technology now allows us to engage with people in opposite parts of the country and the world.

Videoconferencing has now extended to virtual happy hours, career fairs, meet-and-greets, educational webinars, and many more opportunities that can help one grow professionally. I can only imagine how the abundance of today's resources might have helped me pivot in my career back then, but everything in due time, right? I have no desire to repeat the struggles I faced, but I have come to appreciate the lessons and strength I gained from pressing on through those rough patches.

Less Stress and Yet More Stress (Made Worse with Family Duties)

For those who may think working from home is stress-free, think again. Studies show that telecommuting can help ease stress that workers experience in the workplace, but it can also enhance stress in other ways.

True, remote work alleviates stress by eliminating the office commute during rush hour. For example, some telecommuters expressed feeling a stronger sense of well-being and less fatigue than they did when working in an office environment. But like anything else, it comes with its own fair share of hurdles.

Some remote workers experience what scientists call "technostress."[16] Technostress includes work overload, privacy invasion, and unclear deliverables, and the degree to which it affects you depends on how many days a week you work from home. Those who clock in from home less than two and a half days a week are considered "low-intensity" teleworkers, and experience technostress at lower levels than the high-intensity teleworkers who telecommute over two and a half days a week.

Additionally, remote workers—especially those who telecommuted before the pandemic—feel more stressed than they did before. And for those who live with families, the situation is worse. Take Jill Rendelstein, proprietor of J.R. Writing Advantage. A writing coach, writer, wife, and supermom to two amazing children ages ten and thirteen, Jill wages the battle of working while managing her family. Like many moms, the pressure is all too familiar.

"Telecommuting and managing children can take an emotional toll on the psyche," she says. The number of hours the busy mom works varies, depending on the season, ranging from thirty to forty-five hours a week, and every minute is a challenge.

"There is little focus on any task, while I also fail to give the children my full attention," she says. And like many mothers, some of the pressure to perform comes from her own high expectations, which suffer from the wrath of the pandemic.

"I don't feel successful at being a mother or an entrepreneur on these days," she confessed.

And Jill is not alone. Parental stress is at an all-time high—especially for those telecommuters who are now forced to homeschool their children in the wake of the COVID-19 pandemic.[17] According to Pew Research Center, 38 percent of parents with children under the age of twelve described childcare as "difficult" in March 2020, coinciding with the pandemic growing as a hot spot in the United States. Not surprisingly, more women felt the stress of parenting with mothers at 42 percent compared to just 33 percent of fathers. However, six months later, after homeschooling became the norm in many places due to schools, daycare, and other forms of childcare closing, those numbers skyrocketed. As many as 52 percent of parents with children under the age of twelve wrestled with childcare, with 47 percent of fathers and 57 percent of mothers stating they were struggling to care for their children.

Career Limitations—Out of Sight, Out of Mind

As I mentioned earlier, the remote world can amplify the absence of recognition and other forms of absent recognition. It can be more difficult to gain recognition for your work, which is already a challenge in corporate America.

In my second remote job, on too many occasions did I suggest an idea or offer insights that were dismissed only to have them celebrated when another coworker recycled my ideas and presented them as his or her own. Disgruntled, I eventually took the advice of a fellow pharmacist who had telecommuted in nontraditional roles much longer than I: I learned to keep my ideas to myself and protect them for those rare moments when I have would an interaction with a superior. It wasn't easy, but it saved me some additional frustrations down the road.

Becoming Comfortable with the Uncomfortable and the Unknown

Telecommuters and contractors share some commonalities in that they often have to work with limited information. The degree of discomfort one feels can vary on many factors—some internal, others external. Internally, various things, such as personality, values, previous telecommuting experience, degree of self-motivation, and initiative may all contribute to the degree of comfort one experiences with telecommuting. When one can't ask a cube mate or swing by an office for answers, sometimes one has to make educated guesses and judgment calls. I ran into this issue during a call with a suicidal patient. It was a Friday evening and my final patient consultation of the day. The call had run over, and my coworkers, along with my boss, had already left for the day.

No one was available to call or text, and I could not find resources for mental health and suicide management in the protocol manual. Knowing I had another person's life in my hands made me sweat. Of course, I was eager to start my weekend, but I also took an oath and have a conscience. So, I made a judgment call to stay on the line with the patient and console him while trying to identify suicide prevention resources in New York City, where he lived.

Part II

From Surviving Telecommuting to Thriving

Chapter 5

TAKING CARE OF YOUR MENTAL HEALTH

As I mentioned earlier, transitioning from telecommuting one or two days a week to a fully remote position caused me stress and anxiety that I never could have fathomed. I missed even the smallest social interactions. I wanted to socialize. I missed my friends, but as depression settled in, I no longer had the energy to hang out at the end of a long workday. Days would slip away without me even going outside.

It also didn't help that, in an effort to help ease the eyestrain, I began working in the dark. Not only was this move inconsequential for the eyestrain, but it might have made things worse. The company was based on the East Coast, and living in Texas meant starting my workdays an hour earlier. When we were asked to report an hour (and later two hours) earlier, that meant I started my day when it was still dark. Then I would sit in the dark for most of the day. My body became confused, and it took a toll on my hormones. The lack of sunlight and working in the dark surely contributed to my depression. I eventually snapped out of my funk, but it took a lot of personal initiative along with trial and error.

Below are tips I learned on how to recover—and maintain—my sanity.

Managing your social health

If you don't find your social life suffering as a side effect of telecommuting, congratulations. But if you're like me and many other telecommuters I know, you might have to put a little effort into bringing your personal life into balance as a telecommuter.

When I first started telecommuting, I left the house daily, but I soon fell into a hermit trap. To be honest, I don't even know how—or why—it happened. Three or four days would go by without my leaving the house—or even going outside. I have no clue how or why telecommuting somehow diminished my sense of adventure and urge to engage with others, but I ultimately boiled it down to one central concept: If I had no real reason to leave the house, I simply would not.

Remember, unlike today, video calls were not the norm. In fact, my small company didn't even have the software to support video calls. Although I initially dressed in professional attire, as my depression grew, so did my desire to groom myself. As embarrassing as it sounds, I let myself go. Don't get me wrong, I'm a health nut, so I continued to eat well and exercise. It's just I'd stopped putting effort into my physical appearance. After all, who would notice my appearance if I stayed home all day—and several days at that? Once I'd stopped wearing makeup, combing my hair, or dressing up, I found leaving the house required a lot more effort than I wanted to invest.

I had traded in my pumps for flip-flops, my slacks for yoga pants, and my blouses for old college T-shirts—some that I'd slept in the night before. After yoga, I'd shower and put on clean versions of the same uniform. Even though I'd become Ultra-Plain Jane, let's highlight the positive here: At least I continued to shower every day.

Find an accountability partner

Ideally, this would be a trusted colleague from work or someone who teleworks for another company. Schedule weekly coffee chats—virtual or in-person—where you can talk shop and office cooler gossip, if it suits you. If you're a parent, consider scheduling group teleworking dates (if safe in a post-pandemic world) with others in your neighborhood, or scheduling a virtual chat with other working moms and dads. The first event could be an initial meet-and-greet, and depending on its success, you might even consider sharing best practices on homeschooling and parenting while holding down a job.

Create activities calendars for both social and professional events

Developing a social calendar and re-establishing a morning routine of personal grooming and dressing as if I were heading to the office helped me to overcome this hurdle.

Because the week can quickly slip by before you know it, I recommend scheduling social and family calendars at least two or more weeks in advance until finding a groove.

Give yourself a deadline to schedule your events

By Wednesday of each week, any pending plans I have with at least two social events where I network, meet new people, or spend time with friends are confirmed for the following week. I put a reminder on my calendar to make sure I don't slip up. I also require myself to attend at least one professional networking event a month, whether I want to or not. When I feel myself getting lazy and wanting to slip into a routine of inaction, I make it a point to find paid events. The idea of wasting money is incentive enough to get me off the couch!

Since COVID-19, I have also made it a point to schedule meetings with those with whom I feel synergy. Yet another positive outcome of the pandemic is that people seem more open to individual meetings more now than ever before. So, while the pandemic slowed me down in some ways, in others it helped speed things up.

Also, don't just attend events—consider organizing them. For example, you could host or help host happy hour events once or twice a month. Nowadays, even these events can be virtual, if needed. It can be a great way to meet new people, keep in touch with old friends, and de-stress. Plus, it's an excuse to get dressed and get out of that office chair!

Why not offer to plan activities at work? Not only is it a great way to network within your organization, but it is an excellent way to increase visibility and build trust as a team player and leader.

If you are having trouble finding activities to add more balance to your life, I recommend checking out the local entertainment magazines and websites published by independent publishers. For example, when I lived in Austin, I relied on the city's weekly independently published entertainment newspaper, *The Austin Chronicle*, and the Austin360.com website to stay plugged into the action.

When I moved to San Antonio, I traded those resources in for the *San Antonio Current* and MySanAntonio.com. The city's main newspaper also published a weekly insert, in which they highlighted special events and entertainment for the weekend. When I lived in Cincinnati, I relied on *Cincinnati CityBeat* to keep me in the loop. Same thing with Tucson. I think you get the idea. And while this suggestion seems to focus on events and entertainment for single people, these resources often have family-friendly events, too.

Plugging into community events can also be as easy as subscribing to local newsletters and LISTSERVs. Sometimes, these can take time to locate because many are underground and not heavily promoted. But if you keep networking and meeting the right people, you'll quickly come up to speed.

Once your calendar is filled with activities, you might also find more motivation to put some effort into your appearance. After all, you will connect with others outside your home. If you attend video calls requiring you to switch on your camera, you might have the grooming part handled. But after years of wearing yoga pants and free T-shirts from my college days that have seen their best days, I can tell you that having a reason to put on decent clothing can do wonders for your mood.

Take time out for meditation or some other kind of mindfulness practice each day

Yes, I know this sounds very cliché, but meditating or engaging in similar activities can do wonders for your mental health. Studies show that meditation can reduce anxiety, insomnia, pain, and depression, but it is also beneficial for pain and chronic conditions such as high blood pressure.[18]

In order to practice mindfulness, you actually needn't meditate. To illustrate my point: I have maintained a dedicated yoga practice for more than a decade now, and I must confess that, at times, I still have trouble meditating in the traditional sense. I often practice yoga before meditating. A yoga teacher once mentioned the original purpose of yoga was to prepare the body for meditation.

I tend to struggle with meditation due to a very busy mind with a lot of mental chatter. So, besides the physical benefits, I often need to work through a moving meditation before trying to still my mind. There is no such thing as a perfect pose, though I must focus on many nuances in my quest to deepen the practice and connection with my body. As a result, I begin to meditate through the entire practice—literally a moving meditation. That level of concentration allows me to dig deeper, find my own inner silence, and sit with myself.

But everyone is different. I'm sharing what works for me, but if meditation works for you, great. If it's deep belly breathing, wonderful. If it's something else altogether, even better. The main point is that you spend a few minutes each day taking your mind off work. As little as five minutes can work wonders for your mood and concentration. One study found that meditating for even short periods of time improves decision-making as well as mood and stress.[19]

Take the tourist's approach to networking and entertainment

When I moved back to the Houston area after pharmacy school, I discovered much had changed, but many things had also remained the same. I also realized that during my childhood I hadn't participated in many of the cultural events, sights, and activities that were now still available! So, why not take advantage of those opportunities and venture out to enjoy new or traditional features in the area? And of course, many of these activities may be enjoyed alone or with others.

When I wasn't traveling for leisure or work, I made it a point to check out sights and participate in activities I had taken for granted growing up on the outskirts of the city. If you're having trouble getting started, just ask yourself this: 'If I were new to this city or traveling here for the first time, where might I sightsee or connect with others living in the city?' That question is often a good way to get started.

We all have different tastes, so perhaps not all of these activities will appeal to you, but I've listed a sampling of activities below that you can easily find in many cities. Besides being a ton of fun, many of these events are great ways to meet new people and expand your network when such opportunities may seem a bit more limited in a remote working environment.

- **Pick up old hobbies:** At one point, I actually considered attending art school instead of a four-year university. But while I've continued to sketch occasionally, I've unfortunately stopped painting. Around the time I started my full-time remote position, drop-in arts-and-crafts classes were becoming popular in my area. Yet, I didn't have the time to commit to formal art classes, which were typically four-hour classes on a weekday. Even though painting parties aren't geared towards serious artists, it became an outlet that helped me resume my love of painting. And since the parties included supplies, it saved me hundreds of dollars on new art supplies—or taking time to clean up my mess. Not bad for $35–$45 dollars a pop, considering the expense of art supplies.

- **Leave the beaten path:** I'm a firm believer that every city has something special that makes it unique—whether it be a quirky fact, a historical tale, or interesting sights. Over the years, I've really come to appreciate finding hidden gems that add to character and charm to a city. You'd be surprised what you can uncover with a simple Google search. Personally, I enjoy discovering secret tourist attractions where I live or visit. Some of my favorite travel websites include AtlasObscura.com, Tripadvisor.com, and Fodors.com. To be honest, Atlas Obscura has revealed to me more hidden gems than travel books and other standard area resources. Sometimes, simply taking a leisurely stroll or drive can be the easiest way to discover a wonderful attraction that's been right under your nose. So, grab your walking shoes or jump in your car. You'll be surprised at what you find.

- **Art classes:** As I noted earlier, I periodically look into art classes. But most of the classes that interest me require a four-hour block in the middle of my workday. While I don't mind taking an afternoon off during the week now and then, I have found it challenging to make this commitment on a weekly basis. However, your story may be different. Painting "parties," as they are sometimes called (e.g., Painting with a Twist, Pinot's Palette, and other independently owned painting parties), offer one alternative to making such an ongoing commitment. Many of these painting companies cater to those searching for an enjoyable evening—with or without wine. However, they also offer daytime painting classes that families can enjoy together.

- **Wine-tasting classes/events and vineyards:** Whiskey-tasting classes may also be available but are less common. As a native Texan, you can imagine my tremendous disappointment. However, even if you're alcohol averse, visiting vineyards can be a great way to unwind with friends and socialize.

- **Cooking classes:** Although I did not learn to cook until my early 20s, I never thought in a million years I would enjoy cooking classes. However, I must credit my transition to a plant-based lifestyle, which encouraged me to give it a shot. I have taken cooking and food preparation classes in Houston, Atlanta, and even Vancouver, British Columbia, where I actually completed a raw food chef certification course. Not only are cooking classes a ton of fun, but they are also a great way to meet new people. Humans seem to bond over food—regardless of the source.

- **Hiking groups:** I love the outdoors. Not only do hiking groups help me meet my step goals and keep stress at bay, but they often prompt me to meet some amazing people. I also enjoy the informational exchange, as hikers frequently reveal fun life hacks. We also swap information about great places to travel and hike. If you are an introvert or would rather interact with people you already know, you can hike solo or schedule a recurring hike with some friends or coworkers who live in your neck of the woods. Either way, I highly recommend it. And you don't need to be in tip-top shape to enjoy a hike. If you're new to hiking or aren't able to walk on unpaved trails in remote or mountainous areas, start small. Go for a trek around your neighborhood or at a local park. Then, try hiking paved trails before venturing off the beaten path. Like swimming, it's best to hike with a partner—ideally an experienced hiker—and to bring water, trail snacks, a first aid kit, a whistle, and a compass in case the GPS or trail app on your phone fails or loses signal. Check your state park websites for other necessary items, depending on where you hike, area wildlife, and the time of year. For more information about hiking and resources on hiking, check out the following websites and resources:

  - https://www.americanhiking.org is an organization that collaborates with the federal government and various organizations to maintain trails and preserve public spaces for all to enjoy. They also have a database that allows you to search for hiking trails in your area.

- https://www.sierraclub.org:The Sierra Club is one of the oldest hiking clubs in the United States and has chapters in all 50 states as well as Washington, D.C., and Puerto Rico. They are also an environmental organization.

- https://www.meetup.com: Meetup has numerous hiking groups. To find them, all you need to do is search for "hiking" to find hiking groups and related activities.

- **Nature classes at the local arboretum, Meetup, or other facilities:** Having lived in both Houston, Texas, and Cincinnati, Ohio, I now appreciate the variety of classes arboreta offer, such as painting, food preparation, gardening, forest bathing, and plant identification to name a few. They also offer great programming for families and children.

- **Health and wellness workshops:** If you're familiar with the saying "Your health is your wealth," then these types of events can often present new ideas on how to manage your health. I'll attend these events occasionally because I usually leave with some good tips on self-care. Also, if you're interested in these topics, you can often meet like-minded people and make new friends.

- **Conferences and special-interest seminars** (e.g., festivals, yoga conferences, cultural events): Conferences and seminars have always been great ways to meet new people and engage with the community. While many of these events can relate to your line of work, you may also find conferences that cater to your hobbies or interests. And if you really want to shake things up a bit, consider attending an event tied to something about which you know absolutely nothing. You might surprise yourself by stumbling into a new hobby, career venture, or productivity hack.

- **Swimming club or water exercise:** Not only is swimming a total body workout, but it is also a life skill. Regardless of your level, joining a club can help you stay committed by accountability and can be a great way to meet people. When I first arrived in San Antonio, I would drop in on a master class with a guy I was dating who belonged to the group. He was a stronger swimmer than I, and my skills improved tremendously by pushing myself out of my comfort zone. It was awkward at first, but I credit him with helping me become a much better swimmer. He's no longer in the picture, but the lessons he taught have stayed with me. Also, swimming can be a family activity. You can drop the kids off in swim class while you work out. You can find a variety of options that suit your level. And if swimming is not your thing, water aerobics is another good option.

- **Tours on local history and trivia:** Perhaps I'm biased because I occasionally write about history. Honestly, I think tours are a great way to deepen your relationship with an area—whether you have lived there for five years or five minutes. Learning the local history is also a great way to understand more about the culture of the area. As you uncover some trivia, you may also tap into a new place to check out or pass time. For example, it was during a tour of San Antonio's River Walk that I learned about the hiking and biking trails linked to the five missions in the area. (The Alamo is the most famous of the five missions, but the lesser-known ones are hidden gems.) One of those missions offers workshops on arts and crafts, including old school weaving techniques using a traditional weaving loom!

- **Book clubs:** Although I have never joined a book club, some of my friends really appreciate them. They enjoy sharing and hearing other people's perspectives on the book. Trying a book club is on my bucket list, but the free spirit in me has trouble committing to just one book at a time.

- **Writing clubs or other special-interest clubs and groups:** You don't have to write professionally to participate in writing clubs. I belong to several that I drop in on depending on my availability and mood. I rarely use writing clubs for work-related writing. Instead, I use them for creative writing. Knowing others are working on their projects helps me stay motivated. Some writing clubs may offer writing exercises or prompts, and an opportunity to share your work. I recommend doing a little research before dropping in so you know what the program entails. Some groups are paid. Others are free. Like many recreational activities these days, Meetup, Facebook, and local community centers, such as the YMCA, are great places to find these groups. Your local library may also offer a list of book clubs and writing groups in the area. I mention writing here because, even if you're not a writer, writing can serve as a form of therapy. At times, I find it quite cathartic to purge my frustrations with pen and paper. But there are many other groups you can join based on whatever interests you—golfing, fishing, comics, knitting, crocheting, you name it.

- **Programming offered by libraries:** Many of the events libraries offer have either been put on hold or gone remote because of the pandemic, but that doesn't mean you still can't find some activities. I recently signed up for an American Sign Language class offered by my local library. Some libraries present art shows and museum exhibits. If you have the flexibility in your schedule, perhaps you could swing by on an afternoon break.

- **Programs offered by special-interest groups:** Check with organizations that align with your interests to see what sort of special events they are offering.

- **Gym membership or local fitness groups:** In case you haven't noticed already, I've spent a lot of time emphasizing mental health. Physical fitness is no exception because it's good for both your body and your mind. Because it can be so easy to slip into a home hermit phase as a telecommuter, I strongly recommend taking that gym membership a step further and signing up for a class. Not only would it give you something to look forward to, but there's some accountability there. Try to pick something that interests you. That way, you'll stay motivated—even if a friend cannot join you.

Again, I've provided activities based on my personal interests, but this list is not by any means exhaustive. I'm hoping the list I've provided will work as a guidebook to spark ideas to help you create your own experiences.

- **Volunteer:** Volunteering stands alone because of its importance and numerous benefits.

I am passionate about volunteering for several reasons, beyond it filling up my dance card. Not only can I meet like-minded people with potential for networking, but I find helping others can take the focus off my own troubles and help me appreciate your own blessings. Scientific evidence shows that volunteering improves both mental and physical health as well as satisfaction with life.[20] Gratitude and mindfulness are two trendy topics right now, but there is evidence gratitude and mindfulness can relieve stress and boost happiness—not to mention how incredible it feels to help other people.

After recently moving to Montgomery County, Maryland, a few years ago, I was amazed by the number of farms throughout the state, Washington, D.C., and Virginia. I began volunteering at my neighborhood farm as soon as they lifted COVID-19 restrictions. Over time, I found working on the farm helped connect me to my new neighborhood. Since the farm was literally a block away from me, I had absolutely no excuse not to reach out—and I'm forever glad I did.

Farm work gave me a sense of purpose because the staff depended on me as the morning waterer during the hot summer months. After spending hours toiling away at my desk each week, I looked forward to visiting the farm, rolling up my sleeves, and getting dirty.

My grandparents owned a farm, and I'd help out when my parents took me for a visit. Before volunteering at the farm in my neighborhood, most of my farming experience was superficial and noncommittal. As a child, I might sow a few seeds or pick some tomatoes from the family's garden. I'd help my grandpa feed the cows, pigs, chickens, and geese. If we visited during harvesting season, I'd help shell peas and shuck corn, since I was still too short to pick corn. So, working on my neighborhood farm—although much smaller than my grandparents' property—was a completely different experience. I learned sustainable farming practices, composting, mulching, and weeding—all while getting some much-needed vitamin D. Also, the farm often gave us volunteers excess produce they didn't sell—an added bonus, especially since it was organic.

So enough about me. Here are several ways you can find volunteer opportunities. A good place to start is to ask yourself what impassions you? Is there something new you would like to learn? Chances are that an organization supports these interests. Churches, community centers, libraries, shelters, and schools often need volunteers, too.

Sometimes, volunteering starts with a simple ask. For example, I volunteered at the farm after noticing people working there on my daily neighborhood walks. I swung by later with conversation and the rest is history.

Since that time, I've volunteered at additional farms in Washington, D.C., as well as Virginia. It was the perfect way to give back and socialize while staying safe during the pandemic. If you're interested in gardening and there aren't any farms in your area, check for community gardens. If you still have no luck, consider starting your own. And if you happen to live in an apartment or condo without a backyard, look into container and hydroponic gardening. Perhaps your building has a garden on the roof or terrace. One farm I worked on in D.C. actually had a rooftop location, and it reminded me of an apartment I'd toured in Chicago with a rooftop garden. So, be open. You never know what you might find!

In summary, I'm not insistent about your volunteering at a garden—or volunteering at all. But it can be helpful to step outside your comfort zone and try something different.

There are other ways to find volunteer opportunities, too. Some websites provide massive search engines that populate with numerous volunteer opportunities. Examples include:

- https://www.volunteermatch.org/

- https://www.unitedway.org/get-involved/volunteer

- https://www.catchafire.org/volunteer

I have also found volunteer opportunities on Meetup. And believe it or not, the professional networking site LinkedIn sometimes posts volunteer opportunities.

On a professional note, check out professional organizations to which you belong or are considering joining. Their websites may include a volunteer section or announce a call for volunteers. Perhaps they have a committee to which you could lend your services. Consider asking a few friends or close colleagues for suggestions and to share opportunities with you. A serendipitous conversation with a pharmacy mentor resulted in me serving on a committee for the University of Texas at Houston Consortium for Aging, where I helped plan educational activities.

Not only did the opportunity bring me joy and fill my dance card, but my participation brought some added weight to my resume early in my career. I also earned the respect of some of my senior pharmacist colleagues in the process. The moral of the story, in this case, is that being open to new opportunities can help shape your future—an added bonus for the remote worker.

Chapter 6

TAKING CARE OF
YOUR PHYSICAL HEALTH

EVEN if you had an office job prior to the pandemic, it might surprise you how easily you can slip into bad habits, becoming more sedentary in a home office. This is one reason I repeatedly stress the importance of maintaining a workday schedule as well as a personal schedule. If you're naturally driven and self-motivated, maintaining balance in your life may not be an issue for you. If not, I'm happy to share tips to keep you healthy, happy, and fit.

The first thing is to recognize that, whether you work for a large company, a small start-up, or are self-employed, the sheer nature of telecommuting requires more responsibility for your work environment, productivity, work-life balance, and success. While larger companies may have numerous resources available to you, you may have to hunt for or inquire about them. However, regardless of the situation, you'll have to assume a greater sense of responsibility.

Conduct a home ergonomics assessment: In my chemist job, the company required the safety inspector to conduct an ergonomics assessment at my office. He adjusted my chair and computer to make sure that they were at the correct height and alignment to prevent neck and eye strain. I now realize that the company probably employed these policies due to the industrial setting and need to minimize safety risks.

While I must sadly report no such luxuries with any employers since that time, those important lessons stayed with me. You might enjoy a seat on the couch with your computer for a bit, but after a while, your back might hurt because sofas weren't designed for teleworking. Even if you don't notice any issues right away, over time, you may develop discomfort in your body because of working in a position that is not optimal for alignment.

Finding a good office chair can be time-consuming—and expensive. But trust me, it's probably one of the most important investments you can make for your health as a remote worker. Look for a chair with good support for your lower back. Arm rests and neck supports can be helpful, too.

Ideally, you'll test the chair before buying it, but during a pandemic and other situations where shopping and inventory are not as accessible, it might not be so easy. If you're having trouble finding an office chair with good ergonomic features, consider a gaming chair. The colors can be a little over-the-top if you're conservative, or trying to match the chair with the rest of your office, but I've found these chairs are more likely to have ergonomic features. If you decide to invest in a gaming chair, you can also tone down the bright colors with a nice throw or seat cover. There are many standard office chairs with worthwhile ergonomic features, too, but it can be very hit-or-miss.

Kneeling chairs are also an acceptable option to take pressure off your lower back and keep your hips from tightening from prolonged sitting.

Balance or Swiss balls can double as chairs and fitness devices. When I first started telecommuting, I used to sit on one of these babies most of the day. To be fair, I was taking Pilates classes, so it fit into my lifestyle at the moment. Swiss balls can take some getting used to, but they're great for your back and core muscles because they keep you from slumping. In fact, slumping can cause you to fall off the ball. Also, they are great for stretching your back. I enjoy rolling backwards on mine, into a wheel pose, to stretch my chest after a long day at the computer.

Both standing and sit-to-stand desks have surged in popularity before the pandemic. You know an item is trending when they emerge from obscurity to your local Costco warehouse.

As you may have heard, sitting for hours at a time has been shown to increase the risk of heart disease. But did you also know that sitting in positions for long periods of time can also increase your risk for blood clots?

Physical activity: The American Heart Association still recommends children and adults get at least 150 minutes of moderate physical activity in a week or seventy-five minutes of high-intensity aerobic activity.[21] Unfortunately, many people are not moving enough, according to the World Health Organization.[22] And 25 percent of adults are not meeting minimal amount exercise standards.[22] Increasing activity may also prevent as many five million deaths each year.

You're probably well aware that exercise has tremendous benefits for your body and mind, but did you know that physical activity can also help you become a better worker, too? Getting and staying active is a core pillar of achieving and maintaining overall health. Here are a few of the many benefits of exercise:

- It prevents and manages many potentially life-threatening diseases, including heart disease, cancer, and diabetes[21]

- It improves the ability to think, learn, and make sound judgments

- It improves sleep[23]

- It helps us live longer. Since exercise helps fight serious conditions, like heart disease and cancer, being active can add years to your life.

Disclaimer: This section is for informational purposes and does not constitute providing medical or fitness advice. Please talk to your doctor or other qualified healthcare professional before starting any fitness program.

Stretch it out: Everyone feels stiff after remaining in the same position for a long period, even children. I'm sure I don't have to remind you that our flexibility tends to decrease with age. So, we need to preserve it—

and if possible, improve it. Stretching is a wonderful way to do so. There are plenty of books on stretching, but perhaps the easiest resource is the internet. You can easily find YouTube videos with good stretching routines for those long days at the computer.

Here's an example of a YouTube video on stretches for office workers to manage wrist, back, and neck pain: https://www.youtube.com/watch?v=w1INfs260DY

Check out this video for exercises to manage hand and finger stiffness: https://www.youtube.com/watch?v=8SjYDE46qfc

Dr. Levi Harrison, an orthopedic doctor, created the following video to demonstrate a series of stretches to keep one feeling limber throughout the day: https://www.youtube.com/watch?v=db00TEhg9_c

Chair yoga: When I was a little girl, I watched a television show on PBS called *Sit and Be Fit*, where a fit young lady would spend thirty minutes walking viewers through exercises they could do in their chairs. When I first began watching, almost all the people in the audience participating appeared to be senior citizens. So, I thought the show wasn't meant for someone my age. Then, later on, I caught a few episodes with children demonstrating the exercises. Some of the exercises required dumbbells or stretch bands, but I now realize other moves were actually yoga from a chair.

Fast-forward to today, and the tools I learned from watching that program are still relevant. If you haven't heard of chair yoga before, no, your eyes do not deceive you. You actually *can* do yoga from your chair. While some people may think of chair yoga as something only people who are more mature or may use a wheelchair might do, it's actually something anyone of any age can manage. It also works especially well if you spend most of your waking hours sitting at a desk. I've included a few simple chair yoga poses that can help release tension from your back, but of course, there's nothing like a live demonstration. So, I have included links to some short, instructor-guided videos as well.

Below are two chair yoga poses I like to use throughout the day, to stretch muscles and ward off stiffness that comes from hours of sitting.

1. **Cat-cow:** Sit up straight with both feet flat on the floor about hip distance apart. Make sure your back doesn't graze the back of the chair. If necessary, scoot your bottom forward a few inches to allow room for movement for your back. Now, starting from a tall, straight spine and your hands on your knees, tuck your pelvis and let your spine curl like a cow—to a point where you feel a nice, gentle stretch. Your neck should be the last part of your spine to curl. In a similar fashion, move your spine the opposite way. Starting again from the pelvis, roll your pelvis forward. Let the rest of your spine follow the motion like a wave as you arch your back like a cat. Your head should be the last thing to come up. Repeat three to five times, making sure to take long, deep breaths that match your movements. You may want to exhale in the cat stretch and inhale in the cow, and vice versa. I think the most important thing is to just relax, breathe, and listen to your body. Don't push past your edge, but try to relax, and think of the tension melting away from your body as you flow through the movements.

2. **Easy spinal twist:** Starting from the same sitting position with both feet flat on the floor and hip distance apart, sit up straight. You can start from either position, but I'll start with the right. Place your right hand on your left knee. Keeping your spine tall and your right arm mostly straight, begin twisting to your left. Initiate the movement from the bottom of your spine and try not to hunch your shoulders. Continue to focus on sitting tall as you twist, and it's okay to grab the back of the chair with your left hand for support. Try to look over your left shoulder as you twist with a straight spine. Take one or two deep, slow breaths in this position. Then, return to the starting position. Take a breath to realign yourself, making sure your feet are even and that you're starting off with a tall spine. Now twist to the other side, following the same breathing exercises. Repeat three times on each side.

- Eleven-minute chair yoga video: https://www.youtube.com/watch?v=H4SZdq3JSfA

- Seven-minute chair yoga video: https://www.youtube.com/watch?v=QT5hVb82mhM

- Twelve-minute video to release neck tension: https://www.youtube.com/watch?v=6ibGseHwEPQ

Resistance training: If you're older than thirty and reading this book, I probably don't have to tell you your body changes as you age. In fact, once you hit thirty, you can lose between 3 and 5 percent of your muscle mass every decade.[24] And if you have a desk job, that number can rise as high as 8 percent.[25] While you can't stop the clock from ticking or turn back time, there are some things you can do to slow the aging process and reduce the amount of muscle mass you lose as the years pass. Resistance training can help pump the brakes on muscle mass loss and stiffness caused by aging and working at your desk all day.

Several studies suggest resistance training helps slow down muscle mass loss, but the benefits don't stop there. A 2012 study found that just ten weeks of resistance training can boost resting metabolism by 7 percent, decrease fat weight by nearly four pounds (1.8 kg) and add on nearly three pounds of lean body weight. Not only that, but resistance training helps us get around more easily, walk faster, and improves overall physical performance. It also works wonders for self-esteem and cognition. And the benefits still don't stop there. Resistance training may help reduce the risk for diabetes and heart disease. So whip out those stretch bands!

Trampoline jumping/rebounding: As it turns out, trampolines aren't just for kids. Adults can—and probably should—use them, too, if they are able. If you haven't heard, rebounding is a fancy word that describes jumping on a mini-trampoline. Rebounding has long been touted for its alleged health benefits in the integrative and alternative medicine worlds as a way to move the lymph in your body. Lymph is a fluid flowing through a system of vessels called the lymphatic system. Unlike your circulatory system, which relies on the pressure your heart generates from pumping to push blood through the blood vessels of the body, the lymphatic system doesn't have a pressure system to help it circulate. So, it requires extra help to move. Exercise can help circulate lymph, but certain exercises—such as rebounding—are better than others.

Like resistance training, rebounding can help build muscle mass, and it also improves cardiovascular performance. Not only can jumping on a mini-trampoline strengthen your ticker, but it can help you run faster—without the joint-jarring impact of actually running. According to a study published in 2018, people who jumped on a mini-trampoline three times a week for eight weeks became faster runners.[26]

Get your vitamin D: By now, you have probably heard a great deal of information about vitamin D and its effects on the body. There was a time when vitamin D was associated with bone health, but now we know it does so much more than help build and maintain healthy bones. Although we call it "vitamin D," this so-called "vitamin" is actually better described as a hormone. A hormone is a biological compound produced by glands that is responsible for initiating a series of reactions within the human body. Some hormones are often processed through a series of biochemical reactions to convert them into an active form your body can use. Vitamin D is no exception.

As you probably already know, your body can make vitamin D when you expose your skin to sunlight. Certain rays of sunlight, called ultraviolet B, or UVB light, trigger your body to begin the process of making its own vitamin D. However, the body cannot immediately use the UVB rays that land on the skin. First, the UVB goes through a series of steps that involve your liver and kidneys before your body can use the vitamin D. Here's how it works.

When sunlight hits your skin, it stimulates a special kind of cholesterol called 7-dehydrocholesterol to start the process of transforming the vitamin D precursor into something your body can use. In other words, it converts the UVB radiation into previtamin D3. Your skin eventually absorbs this product into your bloodstream, where it travels to the liver and the body begins processing it for use. After the liver finishes processing the hormone, the newly primed vitamin D is then transported to the kidneys, where it undergoes the final step of activation and becomes calcitriol [1,25(OH)2D]—dihydroxyvitamin D, the active form of vitamin D, the body uses.

The sun produces two types of UV light, UVA and UVB. UVA light tends to cause wrinkles and penetrates more deeply into the body's tissues. UVB rays are the most beneficial to the human body because your body makes vitamin D when it absorbs these rays.

If you live in the continental United States, southern states typically have more months of optimal UVB rays and for longer periods each day than people who live in northern states. However, during the winter months, even people living in a place like Arizona where you get sunshine 300+ days a year could benefit from taking a vitamin D supplement during the winter months.[27]

To help illustrate this point, the closer we are to the equator, the longer the peak hours of sun exposure for optimal vitamin D throughout the year. In other words, if you live anywhere above 37 degrees north or below 37 degrees south, you won't receive enough of the sun's beneficial rays to stimulate your body's natural production of vitamin D.[28]

So why am I devoting so much energy to vitamin D? Because we now know that vitamin D does far more than help build strong bones. Studies have shown that those who live in higher latitudes face greater risk for developing heart disease, schizophrenia, infections, and certain cancers.[24] We now understand the link between vitamin D deficiency and a variety of health conditions, including autoimmune conditions such as inflammatory bowel disease and Hashimoto's thyroiditis.

Certain groups of people are at greater risk for vitamin D deficiency. People with dark skin need more time in the sun than a person with fair skin for their bodies to produce the same amount of vitamin D. Kidney and liver disease can also result in lower vitamin D levels. These organs lose the capacity to produce ample vitamin D when they lose some of their function. Those who are homebound, such as folks in nursing homes and/or skilled nursing facilities, are also prone to vitamin D deficiency because they rarely go outside. I can't tell you how many high-dose vitamin D prescriptions I filled for patients in nursing homes who did were not able to go outside very often.

Also, the amount of sunlight needed to produce the required amount of vitamin D depends on your skin tone. Those who are fair-skinned don't need to spend as much time outdoors. However, the darker the skin, the more time needed in the sun for the body to make the same amount of vitamin D as a light-skinned person. Unfortunately, there aren't many good resources on how much sunlight is needed for those with dark skin.

Aim to get outside for a few minutes during peak times, typically between the hours of 10:00 a.m. and 3:00 p.m. (some sources may say between 10:00 a.m. and 2:00 p.m.). I know. I know. You're probably worried about wrinkles or skin cancers such as melanoma. However, to avoid these issues, follow these tips:

1) Get outside during the right time of day (and year); and

2) Do not to stay out in the sunlight too long.

Remember, you just need enough exposure to create the necessary daily dose of vitamin D. The amount the body needs depends on your natural skin color. Fair-skinned people need about twenty minutes in sunlight, while darker-skinned people, such as those of African or South Asian descent, may require a lot more time in the sun to support their overall health.

Also, it's important to note that the optimal times to absorb vitamin D change throughout the year, as well as the time of day. Typically, spring and summer months offer more time each day to absorb UVB light than during fall and winter. Some latitudes are never reached by UVB rays at all.

Check out the shadow your body casts to discover your own optimal vitamin D production hours. A shadow shorter than your height generally means you're outside while the sun is casting more UVB rays than UVA rays. A shadow longer or taller than your body means you're likely outside when the sun is producing mainly UVA rays, which your body cannot use to make vitamin D.

Unfortunately, as mentioned earlier, there is a lack of studies indicating optimum daily vitamin D doses for those with dark skin. So, regardless of your skin tone, please ask a doctor, or other qualified healthcare professional, about sunlight exposure to boost vitamin D levels safely.

Eyestrain: As a person who wears a strong prescription, and has been wearing glasses since the third grade, I've had to learn about eye damage —and eye health—the hard way. Many jobs—whether based at home, in an office, or field setting—require a great deal of screen time. That time obviously comes at a price for your peepers.

Not only are the eyes the windows to the soul, but they are also conduits of eye strain. And sadly, every age group is susceptible, given the increased use of technology across the board.[29] In fact, at least 90 percent of all people who use computers suffer from digital eye strain (DES), also known as computer vision syndrome. DES refers to a spectrum of symptoms, which can include dry eye and trouble with the eyes working together for visual acuity, a condition known as binocular vision dysfunction.[30]

Blue light plays a role, too. By now, you may have heard about the health risks associated with blue light. So, what is it, and why is it harmful?

First off, not all blue light is unhealthy. Blue light from sunlight is natural, but prolonged exposure to blue light—whether artificial or natural —can damage your vision.[31] The sun produces blue light during the daytime. As daylight approaches dusk, blue light rays fade and warmer rays (reds, yellows, and oranges) become stronger. Early man used the shift from blue light to warmer colors as a signal to prepare for sleep. Instinctually, our bodies still react to these cues, but our exposure to artificial blue light from electronics, such as computers, cell phones, televisions, fluorescent and LED lighting, and more, disrupts this natural process, suppressing melatonin—the hormone our body releases that tells us when to fall asleep.[32]

But not only does artificial blue light disrupt sleep, it destroys vision. And children may face the most danger. A study funded by the National Eye Institute found children's eyes actually absorb more blue light from the screens of digital devices than adults.[33]

Dry eye: My eye doctor, whom I've been seeing for more than twenty-five years, has repeatedly warned me about excessive computer use. Users are prone to dry eyes, as they blink less often when staring at a computer screen. The American Academy of Ophthalmology (AAO) echoes my doctor's warnings.[34] You might wonder then, why those who still read actual books and magazines don't complain about dry eye.

According to my optometrist, people who read print books, newspapers, and magazines, blink more frequently than while using a computer. It gives new meaning to the phrase, "Staring at a computer screen all day," doesn't it?

Every time I see my optometrist, he reminds me to take five-minute breaks from the computer after every twenty to thirty minutes staring at the screen.

According to the AAO, humans usually blink fifteen times on average in a minute. The number of blinks plummets 60 percent to five to seven times a minute when we sit down at the computer.[35] Frequent blinking helps prevent headaches, dry eyes, and eyestrain. Use this time to perform some simple eye exercises, such as blinking, eye circles, focusing on objects near and far, and flexing. For examples and instructions on eye exercises to help prevent and manage eyes strain, check out the following resource:

- https://winyatesopticians.co.uk/2018/06/eye-exercises/

So, if you have eyestrain, don't give up. There are several things you can do to find relief.

- **Take breaks.** I've already discussed how taking frequent breaks can help keep you focused and productive. Taking frequent breaks also helps preserve and improve your eye health. The AAO recommends the 20-20-20 rule. This rule means that for every twenty minutes you work, you should stop and stare at something twenty feet away for twenty seconds.

- **Adjust the settings on your monitor to reduce or eliminate blue light.** I happen to use both Mac and PC. Both devices allow customization of user settings to fit personal preferences. A night shift setting on MacBook computers automatically reduces blue light and shifts to warmer colors coinciding with the setting sun in your time zone or based on a time you choose.

If you're an Apple user, both MacBooks and iPhones offer color filters to switch from cooler colors, such as blue, to warmer colors such as red and yellow. I actually use the color filter for my Apple devices so the screens appear black and white like a newspaper. It took a little getting used to at first, but I find that completely removing all blue light has worked wonders for my eyestrain and that my sensitivity has improved. Please note that this is my personal experience. Individual results may vary. And, of course, the black-and-white/color filter setting may not be appropriate for everyone or every job. For example, I restore the color settings when I am working on slide decks or creating graphics, or any content that requires color. However, when I need to restore the color, I use some additional tools to help fight my eye fatigue.

- **Use blue light filters on your computer and cell phone:** If you would rather not tinker with your computer's settings, there are many apps from which you can choose that take the guesswork out. Examples include Night Owl, NightTone, and Screen Colors, which have both free and paid options. I personally use f.lux on my PC. I like it because it is free, works well, and is pretty simple to use. I don't need an app on my Apple devices because I have tweaked their settings, as I mentioned above.

- **Consider blue-light blocking glasses:** I must warn you that traditional blue light-blocking glasses are orange and don't make for the most fashionable eyewear—especially these days when you may find yourself in front of a camera for a Zoom, FaceTime, or Microsoft Teams video call. Fortunately, for those concerned with image, there are at least two other options more aesthetically appealing to the eyes. Consider spending a few extra dollars to invest in a blue light-blocking coating for prescription eyeglasses. Some places, like Costco, offer the coating for free when you purchase your eyeglasses.

- **Perform some eye exercises:** As I mentioned earlier, my eye doctor prescribed a two-minute break with exercises for every twenty minutes I spend staring at my computer screen. Here are some I like, and your blinkers will feel terrific after you finish:

  1. Gaze at an object that is at least twenty feet away for twenty seconds or more. Depending on the size of your workspace, this may mean looking out the window.

  2. Roll your eyes in circles. It doesn't matter in which direction you start, just reverse directions after rolling your eyes ten times, either clockwise or counterclockwise.

  3. Straighten your arm with your index finger raised. Stare at your index finger as you slowly bring it six inches before your face. Now gaze at something twenty feet away. Repeat this exercise five times.

- **Consider downloading apps or software that remind you to take breaks and rest your eyes:** I use eyeCare, which is both MacBook- and PC-friendly. A chime sounds when it's time to take a break, and the settings are easily customizable, depending on how long you want your work sprints to be. It also offers suggestions on eye exercises and physical activities during breaks.

If you have struggled with eye strain after spending hours at the computer, you might also consider making some changes to your diet. Fortunately, these healthy food choices will benefit more than just your eyes.

Berries—especially blue and red ones—contain wonderful antioxidants, such as anthocyanin, which helps shield your eyes from the damage of blue light.[36] Blueberries are great, but bilberry has been shown to have the highest concentration of this eye-saving antioxidant. You can find bilberry supplements sold alone or in combination with vitamins, and other dietary health supplements, which can help preserve eye health.

Consider dietary supplements that support healthy vision: The Age-Related Eye Disease Study 2 (AREDS2) showed that taking the antioxidants lutein (10 mg) and zeaxanthin (2 mg), along with the omega-3 fatty acids DHA (250 mg) and EPA (650 mg), were less likely to progress age-related macular degeneration than those who only took the placebo.[37]

While the AREDS2 study includes two famous omega-3 fatty acids, DHA and EPA, some studies investigating the effects of these, and other fatty acids, on dry eye (which is a symptom of DES) suggest these oils may help either very little or not at all.[38]

Taking supplements is not a magic bullet, so please confer with your doctor, or other qualified healthcare professional first.

Engage in nature: Forest bathing, animal watching, earthing, hiking, canoeing, kayaking, camping, etc., are all great ways to unplug. The benefits of nature cannot be understated—and it provides your eyes with a much-needed break from the computer.

That said, the information I've shared comes from lessons and data I have gathered from my own experience, medical journeys, and research. But if you have questions about managing your health while working from home, please talk to your doctor. Perhaps some of the information I've provided can give you some talking points, but ultimately, your doctor will know what's right for you.

Chapter 7

FROM SURVIVING TELECOMMUTING PSYCHOSIS TO THRIVING

H OPEFULLY, by now you've gathered some wonderful insights on the potential pitfalls of telecommuting, along with some strategies to help prevent or manage them. But technically, this is only one part of the equation—survival. Shifting from surviving to thriving requires a little more effort. Here are some tips to help you work from home efficiently while living your best life.

Strategies to Manage Telecommuting and Children

I realize many of the suggestions I have provided about supporting your physical and mental health as a telecommuter have been from the perspective of a single person. However, that does not make me blind to the special needs of those with families. Remember Jill Rendelstein, an entrepreneur with a husband and a family? Here are her tips to manage your family and your career from home more efficiently.

- Set up play dates or try to involve the children in an activity they can complete alone.

- If possible, schedule time to work for a few hours somewhere away from home. "I work at a friend's home for a few hours a day, when possible, or close the door in a room of our house," Jill says.

- Consider meal prep. The busy mom-apreneur (or dad-apreneur) buys easy, prepped dinners from the market to decrease cooking time and increase time spent with her kids.

- Schedule tasks for the children to complete. If necessary, consider incentivizing them with a reward. For example, Rendelstein asks her children to complete a list of chores and academic activities before they may use screens or see friends.

- And above all, cut yourself some slack. "Be gentle on yourself.... Set small, realistic goals to complete throughout the day," Rendelstein says. "If possible, lighten your workload during these occasions."

Staying Productive and Motivated

Take breaks. Set a timer that chimes every twenty minutes. You might consider using something like the eyeCare app I mentioned in chapter six. You can give your eyes a break while you stand up, stretch, walk around, do jumping jacks, etc.

There are many reasons why twenty-minute sprints are a good working strategy. Everyone is different, but I find that it not only helps me keep track of time but also helps me stay focused. Knowing the clock is winding down encourages me to stay on task, so I know I'm making progress toward my goal when the timer chimes. I take a couple of minutes to stand up and stretch, dance around to an up-tempo song, or do a handstand. With my blood pumping, I return to my desk refreshed, energized, and ready to tackle those deadlines.

Fortunately, the benefits of taking frequent and regular breaks don't end there. Not only can it help you stay productive, but it can help ward off some of the harmful effects of leading a sedentary lifestyle (e.g., increased risk of heart disease, diabetes, and obesity). I have discussed this issue, and more, in the health section (chapters five and six) of this book.

Taking breaks provides more benefits than helping one maintain focus. Studies show that spending too much time seated increases the risk of heart disease, obesity, and other health challenges—even if one exercises regularly. Sure, working out can help keep your ticker strong and your body fit, but a thirty-minute walk or jog cannot fully reverse the effects of sitting for eight hours, when only your eyes and your fingers are moving at the keyboard.

Standing and stretching your body for just five to ten minutes every hour kills two birds with one stone. It provides a moment to recharge, while also reducing your risk for heart disease.

Consider splurging on one guilty pleasure that nourishes your soul. I'm also an avid music lover and musician. Sometimes my break entails dancing to a favorite tune or playing the piano for a few minutes.

I was in the process of relocating just before the COVID-19 pandemic brought the United States to its knees. Life was changing so quickly every day that I wondered if I'd manage to move all my belongings out of storage. Instead of risking detainment while attempting to cross state lines with the rest of my belongings, I sprang for a few hundred bucks on a "replacement" digital piano. Not only does playing bring me comfort during the pandemic, but it helps me unwind and recharge during a stressful workday. While I really didn't want to miss the money, I'm grateful for it every single day and have no regrets.

Network like a boss. Meetup is another great resource to find networking events. In fact, many career, entrepreneurship, and professional networking groups post on Meetup. Join any and all groups that appeal to you. Offer to organize or lead an activity. Not only will this provide additional outlets to look forward to, but it can also increase your chances of expanding your network by becoming more visible—professionally as well. You never know with whom you'll be rubbing elbows and, depending on the organization and task, you can list your leadership role on your resume.

Other professional networking apps and/or websites include Clubhouse, Shapr, LinkUp, and Alignable. However, they have not been around as long as LinkedIn, which now boasts nearly one billion users, last I heard.

Separate your workspace from the rest of your living quarters. Much like this country was founded on a separation of church and state, your work and homelife should be separate, too. Even though it sounds simple, I cannot stress enough the importance of creating a workspace independent of where you spend your nonworking hours. If you have the space for it, use a separate room as your office and *do not* use it for anything else.

When I began my first fully remote position, I converted a barely used room in the house into my home office. When I logged off each day, I closed the door—and I rarely opened it until it was time to go back to work.

Setting Boundaries with Friends and People Who Live with You

Last year, a good friend of mine and I reconnected. We had lost touch after she remarried a few years ago. Before she remarried, we would talk almost every day. It thrilled me to pick up where we left off, but I also noticed that she seemed oblivious to my time and work schedule.

"You must think I'm a lady of leisure," I said with a forced chuckle, hoping she'd catch the hint. I was happy to chat but had become extremely annoyed that she rarely called in the evenings when I was much less likely to be working.

"Oh girl, you work from home," she said, laughing. "So, you can work whenever."

While her statement is technically true, the idea of working "whenever" isn't exactly the best idea when it comes to time management and quality of life. As stated in previous chapters, some people may actually need to work from home themselves before fully understanding your situation. Regardless, set your boundaries, and set them early. Otherwise, you set yourself up for abuse.

Boundaries are physical as much as they are emotional and psychological. This is another reason to establish that home office closed off from the rest of the house. However, those boundaries must be softened in certain situations, such as when you are caring for small children or a sick relative. In these and other situations, creating a complete physical barrier may not be possible, and you must work to find a strategy that allows you to meet your familial needs while remaining productive. However, whenever you can establish those boundaries, it helps others—including the IRS for those of you who are independent contractors—to view your working environment differently.

Switch it up. Change up your work setting. Call me OCD if you will, but I confess I have an obsession with rearranging furniture. I'm not sure why, but I think part of it is the excitement of giving the same space a new look, and therefore, a new feel.

I will also admit that my rearranging fetishes seem to have gotten worse during the pandemic. In the first six months, I rearranged my office space five times alone! I can admit that probably sounds extreme, but I needed to reimagine my office after spending more time at home than usual— probably because of the pandemic and sheltering in place.

But you don't have to give your office space a massive makeover to give it a boost. Something as simple as hanging up a picture, a brightly colored office chair, or new curtains can work wonders for your mood and productivity.

Of course, we all have our personal preferences, but if and when redecorating, I encourage you to consider carefully the colors you choose. Believe it or not, colors can have a powerful effect on your mood. And certain colors—such as gray, beige, dark blue, and black—can actually cause depression.

I was excited to move into an apartment with an accent wall in my office space. However, I also cringed at the color it was painted—you guessed it —a dark grayish-blue. Because I have brown skin with yellow undertones, the color might be a significant contrast against my complexion during video calls with clients and friends. But I'll be the first to admit the color disturbed me at first. Decorating the office with vibrant complementary colors was a perfect solution.

My corner desk is tan. A tall white bookshelf livens up the wall on video calls. I bought a beautiful orange pot to repot my peace lily and a yellow pot for one of my crispy air ferns. I also purchased a printer with the same undertone but in a lighter shade than the wall. Even my vacuum cleaner is orange. Not only is the contrast visually appealing, but it takes the edge off what would otherwise be a very depressing room to spend eight hours a day.

Another thought is to add an office plant or two, if you haven't already. Not only do plants help filter the air, but indoor gardening in any capacity can work wonders for your mental health. Believe it or not, adding a touch of greenery to your office can reduce stress.[39] However, some of the most common indoor plants are actually quite poisonous. So, as a general rule of thumb, make sure you keep your children and pets away from these and other plants—just in case.

I strongly encourage you to spend a little time Googling indoor plants, their properties, and their care before settling on what to buy. Also, if you're new to gardening or have a brown thumb, consider a hearty plant that requires minimal care and can survive abuse and neglect (not to say that you would intentionally neglect your plant).

In 1989, the National Aeronautics and Space Administration (NASA) collaborated with the Associated Landscape Contractors of America on what became known as the Clean Air Study.[40] The goal of the study was to identify plants that do a good job of purifying indoor air. They tested numerous plants and found some that several have a strong ability to improve air quality to improve air quality by removing carbon dioxide, carbon monoxide, formaldehyde, benzene, trichloroethane, and other toxins from an enclosed environment.

Researchers found several houseplants—many of which have tropical origins—that do wonders for air purification. I've picked out a few that are easy to grow and make beautiful additions to your home office and your home overall. Most of these nature gems made NASA's clean air list, too.

Aloe vera *(aloe barbadensis, aloe africana)* are hearty plants, good air purifiers, and are easy to grow. They require little water or sunlight and take a lot of talent to kill. Aloe vera produces a gel that is both medicinal and cosmetic. When the leaves are broken, the gel makes a great first aid option to soothe minor burns. Aloe vera gel can also be used with hair products. Some cultures ingest aloe vera gel for digestive complaints, but I would not recommend doing this without the guidance of a qualified healthcare professional. I would also warn against using aloe vera gel for any other use without medical advice. Despite its soothing properties, some people may find it irritates their skin. Also, aloe contains a form of latex that increases the risk for side effects if you're taking certain medications, such as digoxin, which doctors often prescribe for heart problems.[41]

The **peace lily** is also a great air purifier, but it can be fussy. Watering can be tricky, as they may droop from over- or under-watering. However, they still require regular watering in a pot and good soil drainage. They prefer humid environments. However, once you get the hang of it, peace lilies make striking additions to an office—especially when they bloom. Some people oil the leaves to bring shine, but I find the leaves carry their own inviting gloss when the plant is healthy and well-nourished. Please note, peace lilies are toxic. So, while you probably wouldn't snack on them, make sure your small children and pets steer clear, too.

Crispy air ferns have a fun texture and are also easy to grow. They thrive on humidity and water. You'll know right away when these plants feel abused. Their leaves will turn brown and shrivel, and they may even start to pale. These signs are usually clear indicators the plants need more water. They also like to grow to accommodate the size of their container, so don't be surprised if these babies take over whatever pot they're in. And remember, the bigger the plant, the more zen you'll bring to your office, not to mention filtering more air.

If you believe in luck and prosperity, plants such as **bamboo** and **money trees** are said to help in both these categories. One of my favorites is the *Zamioculcas zamiifolia* family, commonly known as the **ZZ plant** or **Zanzibar gem**, named after East African country Tanzania from which it originates. The ZZ plant does a great job of filtering toxins from the air. Also, it's great for people new to gardening or who have trouble growing plants because it grows well with minimal watering, sunlight, and attention. It sounds crass, but the plant usually thrives despite neglect. Unless I've recently repotted them, I only water mine about once a month, and they are completely happy. The major drawback with the ZZ plant is needing to repot them fairly frequently because they multiply. Sometimes, one plant multiplies into five or six individual plants with new bulbs. This can be both a blessing and curse, depending on whether you want more plants and have the space to repot new bulbs. Overall, ZZ plants offer a great bang for your buck because you might end up with several plants after purchasing just one. Plus, with their smooth, naturally glossy leaves and overall enchanting appearance, it's hard not to fall in love with these babies.

Please note that, while all these plants help filter the air, they won't remove all toxins. Some plants remove certain toxins, but maybe not others. Please research the environmental pollutants removed by indoor plants before making a selection.

Some great websites and resources for indoor gardening are:

- https://landscapeforlife.org

- https://gardenista.com

- https://www.motherearthnews.com

- https://thehouseplantguru.com

- https://commongardenground.com

I also suggest reading a blog written by my friend, Chris Abdo, an Austin-based horticulturist. I am sharing this information in full transparency, as he did not ask me to promote his site. However, I have come to him with plant questions quite frequently, and he always helps me get back on track.

In fact, if you search his website (https://commongardenground.com), you'll notice a video I sent him to help me revive my peace lily: (https://commongardenground.com/2020/11/11/how-to-know-if-a-plant-needs-waterthe-big-list/)! Since his gardening tips have worked for me, I think they can work for you, too. Chris also grows much of his own food and shares wonderful tips on both indoor and outdoor gardening.

Even if houseplants are not your thing, a cheap imposter from Marshalls or Target will do, too.

Motivational music: I love all kinds of music—perhaps because I am a musician myself. That said, just because I like many genres doesn't mean they all motivate or help me stay on task. In pharmacy school, I could only study to opera or jazz. I found both to be relaxing and stimulating at the same time.

Nowadays, I goof off when I hear some of this music, so I have switched to music designed for concentration. I know it sounds boring and methodical, but I have noticed this music helps me focus. I wouldn't recommend playing this kind of music on a road trip, but you can find plenty of free music for work, concentration, and studying on YouTube or you can subscribe to something like Brain.fm. They offer a free trial before a paid subscription.

These days, high-frequency music helps me stay on task while boosting my energy. Although I haven't found any studies supporting my findings, I feel uplifted and ready to focus when I play this kind of music. If you try this route, find music that's at least 528 Hz in frequency or greater.

Staying focused also plays a critical role in helping you reclaim a social life. Some remote jobs have flexible hours provided you are productive. But having some wiggle room in the schedule that allows you to make up time lost in the evenings can backfire if you can't stay on task. Goofing off may seem like fun, but it normally catches up with you when working remotely.

The Total Package: Finding Your Own Personal Telecommuting Groove

As I've stated throughout this book, I am not offering medical advice or pretending I have all the solutions to maintaining your sanity in a world of chaotic telecommuting. My hope is that by sharing my personal story, struggles, and triumphs, you can learn from my mistakes and successes. Use what serves you, and omit the rest.

So, as you continue working remotely, you'll fall into a groove that works for you. I hope that this book has offered you some tools, and perhaps inspired you to find your own system. After all, we are all different, so what works for me for may not work for you. And sometimes, what once worked may stop being as effective.

Over the years, I've noticed that even when we find a groove, sometimes our routine could use a tune-up or even a full makeover. Pre-COVID pandemic, my tune-up or recharge came from incorporating travel and assuming a digital nomadic lifestyle that allowed me to work and travel in different locations. Essentially, I drew inspiration from altering my surroundings.

The change of environment helped to stimulate and maintain my focus. During the pandemic, though, I chose to shelter in place—even several weeks before the federal government asked us to stay at home. For the first time in nearly a decade, I was stagnant. The psychological renewal and adventure I had previously enjoyed from a change of scenery vanished. The mental side effects felt like déjà vu—eerily echoing what I'd previously experienced as a newbie telecommuter. In the same way I had to handle the fallout of telecommuting and feeling isolated, I had to figure out how to keep life fresh during lockdown.

Fortunately, telecommuting 2.0 for me was not as isolating. I now had millions of Americans experiencing the same tough issues with me. For the first time since I'd become a full-time remote worker, I had a community of people who did not question my sanity. More people than ever seemed to get it, to understand what I was enduring—even if they still had never telecommuted. Suddenly, they had a significant other, relative, or friend who worked from home. Somehow, the personal connections made the nuances of telecommuting more relatable.

Mastering the Zoom (or Microsoft Teams) Call

I have a confession. I will be the first to say I am not the biggest fan of video calls, but this is mainly because I already enjoyed a solid work routine before the pandemic introduced millions of first-time telecommuters into the work environment.

I find video calls are less efficient because they prevent me from multitasking as I had while meeting via phone. Also, more meetings have now cropped up in the pandemic-induced, mass remote era. Pre-COVID, video meetings for me were rare, and they were mainly for job interviews. For example, I had several interviews with various pharmaceutical companies via video—and one interviewer was overseas. The ability to experience a human moment with someone on another continent thrilled me. I will confess that I made many mistakes with my first video calls. Some mistakes were simple—such as poor lighting or having the camera at an unflattering angle. Others were not as obvious, like testing the videoconferencing software to see confirm that the noise-canceling features muted out distractions in the background. But as with telecommuting, I earned the battle scars so you don't have to.

The deluge of new telecommuters has also created a level of compassion for interruptions and disturbances previously viewed as taboo, unprofessional, and downright unacceptable. For instance, one would have been harshly judged by background noise coming from a child or pet. Watching a child innocently barge into an office space and appear on camera was previously the ultimate faux pas. Now, the homeschooling uptick also caused by the COVID-19 pandemic has made these types of inconveniences forgivable, acceptable, and sometimes laughable.

I will admit, I occasionally feel a twinge of jealousy from the positive feedback and overwhelming support people in these environments now receive on social media. At one point in my telecommuting career, I juggled my job and my mother, who had an amazing gift for barging into my office with requests right in the middle of a professional phone call. And yes, these—and other interruptions—showed up in my performance review.

Ultimately, the pandemic has taught us that we are all human, and we can all face very human experiences despite being professionals. At the end of the day, we all want to put our best faces forward. So, here are my tips for remaining as professional as home life allows when on camera.

Pimp your office space. You don't need to spend a ton of money fashioning your home office into an executive suite, but the area appearing on camera should be clean, organized, and clear of clutter.

Virtual backgrounds are a great way to conceal the clutter, but it never hurts to be prepared for random moments when technology fails and your virtual background reveals "the man behind the curtain." (I've had it happen.) But making a few simple changes to your background not only helps boost the viewer's perception of your professionalism, but it can make your home office feel more authentic, too.

Granted, the viewer on the other end is there to see you, but these days, putting your best foot forward on camera transcends perfectly coiffed hair, polished makeup, and a clean shirt. It also means you want to portray a professional environment—even if that environment also doubles as your residence.

I recently bit the bullet and invested in a bookcase upgrade. I hated to spend the money, but all the compliments on my background and questions about its authenticity are confirmation I did the right thing.

So, a bookcase with politically neutral books, a lovely potted plant, or a delightful picture can make for an inviting background. And sometimes less is more. I've seen some great backgrounds with plain white walls and only offset by an accent photo.

Find good lighting. I have a strong aversion to darkness, so I struggle with dark colors and poor lighting. As it turns out, these pet peeves are helpful when prepping for a video call. We all want to be seen in our best light—both literally and figuratively. In the literal sense, light—and especially natural light—can be your very best friend. If you can swing it, find a room with large windows to let the natural light shine. And if that room happens to be on the east side of the house, try to schedule video calls before noon to take advantage of nature's golden rays.

Not only is the natural light good for hormonal balance and keeping our circadian rhythms on track, but it also enhances our appearance on camera. Natural light has a way of washing out imperfections. Blemishes fade, and wrinkles disappear. It gives the skin a magical glow. Even without the advantage of great natural lightning, there are lightbulbs on the market that will simulate their effects. I use them in office lamps.

Get a Ring Lamp. With so many Instagrammers, TikTokkers, and YouTubers out there, the demand for ring lamps has increased. I will confess I waited years to purchase one, but I am glad I did. A colleague finally talked me into it. Since she once worked for Black Entertainment Television, I thought I should listen. I'm happy I did. I still swear by natural light, but natural light and ordinary indoor lighting do not always eliminate shadows. A ring lamp is shaped like a ring, and beautifully erases shadows from your face. In other words, it literally paints you in your best light!

If warranted, consider investing in a quality headset. While it's true that most computers now have decent cameras and microphones, a quality headset can make a significant difference in your experience for filtering out background noise and assuring your voice comes through clearly. Visually, headphones can improve an already professional image, creating a more serious air. Some will include noise-canceling audio, protect your hearing with lower volumes, but can increase productivity by silencing distractions—such as kids or television playing in another room.

Staying "Visible" While "Invisible" Offer to take on leadership roles. All too often in our society we associate leadership with management, but there are many ways to demonstrate leadership beyond having direct reports. Offer to take on additional work if you have the bandwidth. Contribute new ideas or offer solutions to a recurring pain point. As I mentioned earlier, you can also offer to help with various initiatives.

For example, perhaps you have a skill set beyond your core duties that could benefit the company. With more companies offering health and wellness programs due to the surge in new telecommuters, you could organize a workshop on self-care. If you're a yoga instructor, perhaps offer to teach a virtual yoga class. If you are an authority in health and wellness or have a background in personal training, you could share fitness tips with HR to incorporate in the company's newsletter. Maybe you want to share some quick, healthy recipes for fellow employees who are juggling full-time teleworking with full-time homeschooling and babysitting. The list goes on and on.

Recognize that some strategies to gain recognition for your home-based work may look different than if you were in the office. Many strategies of meaningful contribution look the same. At the end of the day, work is work. You still have deadlines to meet, projects to deliver, presentations to give, meetings to attend, and customers to serve. So, whatever your job, the work does not cease. But sometimes, the visibility and credit for your work fade into the abyss.

And yet again, we have COVID-19 to thank for removing some of the guesswork from solving the issue of receiving recognition for your value. Instead of wondering about your coworker's face and mannerisms, we now also use amazing technology to help us see one another by video and connect.

Be vocal… but not too vocal. But please, don't talk just to hear yourself talk or be noticed. Trust me, if you're one of those folks making quips on the ends of everyone else's statements, people will notice—and some will be annoyed. Sometimes, silence is okay, too.

Be smart and strategically vocal. I say this because the office environment can be a bit cutthroat at times. I have repeatedly heard my ideas downplayed or ignored, only to witness them recycled in meetings from the mouths of coworkers, who stole the idea and received credit and praise.

Keep some secrets for yourself. Before you gasp and say, "Frieda, that's cold-blooded!" Consider this: If you give *everything* away, you'll have no more to give and therefore, nothing to sell. Are you familiar with the phrase, "Leave them begging/wanting for more"? This is a strategy successful recording artists have used for years. Think of it as calling Bruno Mars back on the stage for an encore performance. For example, before I became an independent consultant, I had a coworker call me and pick my brains for intel on how to solve some of the communication hurdles our team was facing with the patients we served. I shared many hard-learned lessons openly, but I saved the biggest and most important piece of information for our next team meeting. As I suspected, my colleague presented the recommendations I'd given him as his own. Fortunately, at the next meeting, two tiers of management were present, and I revealed some of my other tried-and-true tips then. This helped to elevate the respect for my unique skill set and reinforce my value to the team. Meanwhile, I preserved my colleagues' respect as a team player.

As I mentioned in other chapters, receiving credit for work and ideas is important in the workplace, especially in the remote setting.

Now, how you call attention to your work will be up to you. It's specific to each industry. Schedule monthly check-ins with your boss. Network with others in your company who work in roles in which you're interested, or who hold influence and connections to help you progress to the next level. Tell potential stakeholders about the work you're doing.

Fortunately, technological advancements have made it easier to see and be seen. For example, if your company uses Microsoft Teams, you probably know it has many more resources beyond video meetings to improve cross-functional and team-based collaboration. If it's appropriate, consider creating a folder displaying your finished project that supports other team members and people in the organization. Chat a general "hello" just as meetings begin to let people know you're in attendance. Ask team members and stakeholders what help looks like to them. Get the idea? The strategies are similar to what you would use in an in-house setting. The only thing really changing is the execution.

The Telecommuting Anti-Psychosis Employer Screening Questionnaire

As with any job, there will always be some situations you either cannot avoid or did not see coming. You will just have to roll with the punches. However, because some situations are unique and differ greatly from an in-house or field role, the better prepared you are for the situation, the better off you'll be.

It's important to recognize that part-time or freelance telecommuting gigs may not carry the same challenges or stress of full-time telecommuting. After all, you may not depend on those roles for opportunity or growth, and being a non-salaried employee or contractor always changes relationships and expectations on both ends.

Full-time telecommuters who are new to telecommuting may be in for a rude awakening. But you can absorb some of the shock beforehand with a little preparation and collection of important information about the role and the employer.

Here are some tips to help create a positive and more productive working environment. Like many things in the business world, it's important to negotiate as much as possible while the offer is on the table. Once you accept, so many details become inflexible. To solve this issue, I've included a questionnaire to help you gather important information and consider various employers and offers in this employee's market.

1. Find as much information as possible about the company, the culture, your role, and the working environment.

2. Look for employer red flags. This is perhaps most important during the recruitment phase because once you're hired, the opportunity to negotiate usually closes or becomes extremely limited.

   - Is the role clearly defined? If not, why?

   - Does the job description align with the interview proceedings and your perception of the role?

- Does the employer seem to conceal certain information that might indicate the role is either hard to fill or has a high turnover rate?

- Do you gather a sense of urgency? If so, what support mechanisms does leadership have to ensure you receive adequate onboarding while setting realistic deadlines for your deliverables?

3. Ask the right questions.

- Ask your boss about their management style.

- How many employees does your boss manage, and do they all have roles similar to yours? If not, what are their roles?

- How many remote workers does your boss manage?

4. Training and Development

- Find out what training is offered. If training seems limited, try to negotiate for training opportunities with your hiring manager. Of course, in order to seal the deal, you'll need to justify how the investment will benefit the company.

- What are the opportunities for growth and advancement?

- Does the organization offer mentorship or leadership and development programs?

- Find out how the employer sees your role evolving over time.

- How will the employer evaluate your performance and deliver feedback?

- What are the salary expectations?

5. Degree of travel, department interaction, and cross-functional relationships

- Does this role involve travel? If so, how much?

- If this role is remote, how will you engage with your coworkers?

- If the role requires minimal to no travel, are there team-building events or annual meetings that allow you to engage with your coworkers?

- Will the department hold weekly meetings or check-ins? How will the meetings be conducted (phone, video, etc.)?

- What measures does the organization use to maintain a positive, productive, and engaging work culture for its teleworkers?

Looking Forward

It is my sincere hope that this book helped you in some way, shape, or form—even if only with one takeaway. As I've said before, I don't claim to have all the answers, but I do claim to offer some solutions by sharing what has worked for me and the evidence behind some of these claims. As you continue on your telecommuting journey, you will find your own rhythm—with or without this book. Regardless of how you achieve your teleworking goals, I support and applaud you for seeking answers.

Thank you for letting me be a part of your journey. I wish you health, prosperity, and telecommuting *anti*-psychosis.

Endnotes

1. PubMed. (n.d.). Retrieved October 10, 2020, from https://pubmed.ncbi.nlm.nih.gov/?term=\%28telecommuting\%29+AND+\%28mental+health\%29\&sort=

2. Mann, S., & Holdsworth, L. (2003). The psychological impact of teleworking: Stress, emotions, and health. *New Technology, Work and Employment, 18*(3), 196-211. https://onlinelibrary.wiley.com/doi/abs/10.1111/1468-005X.00121

3. Herring, T. (2020). The research is clear: Solitary confinement causes long-lasting harm. *Prison Policy Initiative.* https://www.prisonpolicy.org/blog/2020/12/08/solitary_symposium

4. Statista. (n.d.). Change in remote work trends due to COVID-19 in the United States in 2020. Retrieved October 10, 2020, from https://www.statista.com/statistics/1122987/change-in-remote-work-trends-after-covid-in-usa/

5. Kelly, J. (2020, May 19). After announcing Twitter's permanent remote work policy, Jack Dorsey extends same courtesy to Square employees. *Forbes.* https://www.forbes.com/sites/jackkelly/2020/05/19/after-announcing-twitters-permanent-work-from-home-policy-jack-dorsey-extends-same-courtesy-to-square-employees-this-could-change-the-way-people-work-where-they-live-and-how-much-theyll-be-paid/?sh=7ec3f6aa614b

6. Global Workplace Analytics. (2021, June 22). Telecommuting trend data. http://globalworkplaceanalytics.com/telecommuting-statistics

7. Krumrie, K. [2016, July 16]. *Why you consider letting your employees work remotely.* https://www.ziprecruiter.com/blog/why-you-should-consider-letting-employees-work-remotely/

8. Cage, A. (2021, October 27). *The great American walkout.* National Fund for Workforce Solutions. https://nationalfund.org/great-american-walkout/

9. Henke, R. M., Benevent, R., Schulte, P., Rinehart, C., Crighton, K. A., & Corcoran, M. (2016). The effects of telecommuting intensity on employee health. *American Journal*

of Health Promotion, 30(8), 604-612. https://doi:10.4278/ajhp.141027-QUAN-544

10. Goolsby, A. (2021, September 8). The battles to come over the benefits of working from home. *The New York Times.* https://www.nytimes.com/2021/07/20/business/remote-work-pay-bonus.html

11. Minkin, R. (2021, January 25). *Even in industries where majorities can telework, some face challenges working from home during the pandemic.* Pew Research Center. https://www.pewresearch.org/fact-tank/2021/01/25/even-in-industries-where-majorities-can-telework-some-face-challenges-working-from-home-during-pandemic/

12. Zeidner, R. (2020, March 21). *Coronavirus makes work from home the new normal.* Society of Human Resource Management. https://www.shrm.org/hr-today/news/all-things-work/Pages/remote-work-has-become-the-new-normal.aspx

13. Oakman, J., Kinsman, N., Stuckey, R., Graham, M., & Weale, V. (2020). A rapid review of mental and physical health effects of working at home: How do we optimise health? *BMC Public Health, 20*, 1825. https://doi.org/10.1186/s12889-020-09875-z

14. State of Remote Work. (2019). State of remote work 2019. *Buffer.* Retrieved April 10, 2021, from https://buffer.com/2021-state-of-remote-work

15. Human Resources Director. (2013, April 30). *US executives see telecommuting as an avenue to career stagnation.* https://www.hcamag.com/ca/news/general/us-executives-see-telecommuting-as-an-avenue-to-career-stagnation/125076

16. Oakman, J., Kinsman, N., Stuckey, R., Graham, M., & Weale, V. (2020). A rapid review of mental and physical health effects of working at home: How do we optimise health? *BMC Public Health, 20*, 1825. https://doi.org/10.1186/s12889-020-09875-z

17. Igielnik, R. (2021, January 28). *A rising share of working parents in the U.S. say it's been difficult to handle child care during the pandemic.* Pew Research Center. https://www.pewresearch.org/fact-tank/2021/01/26/a-rising-share-of-working-parents-in-the-u-s-say-its-been-difficult-to-handle-child-care-during-the-pandemic/

18. National Center for Complementary and Integrative Health. (n.d.). Meditation: In depth. Retrieved April 11, 2021, from https://www.nccih.nih.gov/health/meditation-in-depth

19. Creswell, J. D., Pacilio, L. E., Lindsay, E. K., & Brown, K. W. (2014). Brief mindfulness meditation training alters psychological and neuroendocrine responses to social evaluative stress. *Psychoneuroendocrinology, 44*, 1-12. https://www.sciencedirect.com/science/article/abs/pii/S0306453014000584

20. Yeung, J.W.K., Zhang, Z., & Kim, T. Y. (2018). Volunteering and health benefits in general adults: Cumulative effects and forms. *BMC Public Health, 18*(1), 8.

https://www.sciencedirect.com/science/article/abs/pii/S0306453014000584

21. American Heart Association. (2018). American Heart Association recommendations for physical activity in adults and kids. *Heart Attack and Stroke Symptoms*. https://www.heart.org/en/healthy-living/fitness/fitness-basics/aha-recs-for-physical-activity-in-adults

22. World Health Organization. (2020, November 26). *Physical activity*. https://www.who.int/news-room/fact-sheets/detail/physical-activity

23. MedlinePlus. (n.d.). Benefits of exercise. *National Library of Medicine*. Retrieved July 12, 2021, from https://medlineplus.gov/benefitsofexercise.html

24. Harvard Health Publishing. (2016, February 19). Preserve your muscle mass. https://www.health.harvard.edu/staying-healthy/preserve-your-muscle-mass

25. Westcott, W. L. (2012) Resistance training is medicine: Effects of strength training on health. *Current Sports Medicine Reports,11*(4), 209-216. https://doi.org/10.1249/JSR.0b013e31825dabb8

26. Witassek, C., Nitzsche, N., & Schulz, H. (2018). The effect of several weeks of training with minitrampolines on jump performance, trunk strength and endurance performance. *Dtsch Z Sportmed, 69*, 38-44. doi:10.5960/dzsm.2018.318

27. Jacobs, E. T., Alberts, D. S., Foote, J. A., Green, S. B., Hollis, B. W., Yu, Z., & Martínez, M. E. (2008). Vitamin D insufficiency in southern Arizona. *American Journal of Clinical Nutrition, 87*(3), 608-613. https://doi.org/10.1093/ajcn/87.3.608

28. Harvard Health Publishing. (2021, September 13). Vitamin D and your health: Breaking old rules, raising new hopes. https://www.health.harvard.edu/staying-healthy/vitamin-d-and-your-health-breaking-old-rules-raising-new-hopes

29. Sheppard, A. L., & Wolffsohn, J. S. (2018). Digital eye strain: Prevalance, measurement and amelioration. \textit{BMJOpenOphthalmol}, *3*(1), e000146. https://doi.org/10.1136/bmjophth-2018-000146

30. Coles-Brennan, C., Sulley, A., & Young, G. (2019). Management of digital eye strain. *Clinical and Experimental Optometry, 102*(1), 18-29. https://doi.org/10.1111/cxo.12798

31. Chang, A. M., Aeschbach, D., Duffy, J. F., & Czeisler, C. A. (2014, December 22). Evening use of light-emitting eReaders negatively affects sleep, circadian timing, and next-morning alertness. *Proceedings of the National Academy of Sciences of the United States of America, 112*(4), 1232-1237. https://doi.org/10.1073/pnas.1418490112

32. Prevent Blindness. (n.d.). *Blue light and your eyes*. Retrieved January 20, 2022, from https://preventblindness.org/blue-light-and-your-eyes/

33. http://www.ncbi.nlm.nih.gov/pubmed/21600300?report=abstract

34. Vimont, C. (2021, March 10). Should you be worried about blue light? *American Ophthalmology.* https://www.aao.org/eye-health/tips-prevention/should-you-be-worried-about-blue-light

35. Sheppard, A. L., & Wolffsohn, J. S. (n.d.). Digital eye strain: Prevalence, measurement and amelioration. *BMJ Open Ophthalmology,* 3(1). Retrieved February 1, 2021, from https://bmjophth.bmj.com/content/3/1/e000146?fbclid=IwAR0SlDlCrj55y3Y_NznrAWeWq6TvDKP7LpAvZ5Li2R4gMVaPP72kErx2T0g\&int_source=trendmd\&int_medium=cpc\&int_campaign=usage-042019

36. Ogawa, K., Kuse, Y., Tsuruma, K., Kobayashi, S., Shimazawa, M., & Hara, H. (2014). Protective effects of bilberry and lingonberry extracts against blue light-emitting diode light-induced retinal photoreceptor cell damage in vitro. *BMC Complementary Alternative Medicine, 14,* 120. https://doi.org/10.1186/1472-6882-14-120

37. Age-Related Eye Disease Study 2 Research Group. (2013). Lutein + zeaxanthin and omega-3 fatty acids for age-related macular degeneration: The Age-Related Eye Disease Study 2 (AREDS2) randomized clinical trial. *JAMA, 309*(19), 2005–2015. https://doi.org/10.1001/jama.2013.4997

38. Downie, L. E., Ng, S. M., Lindsley, K. B., Akpek, E. K. (2019). Omega-3 and omega-6 polyunsaturated fatty acids for dry eye disease. *Cochrane Database of Systematic Reviews, 12*(12), CD011016. https://doi.org/10.1002/14651858.CD011016.pub2

39. Lee, M. S., Lee, J., Park, B. J., & Miyazaki, Y. (2015). Interaction with indoor plants may reduce psychological and physiological stress by suppressing autonomic nervous system activity in young adults: A randomized crossover study. *Journal of Physiological Anthropology, 34*(1), 21. https://doi.org/10.1186/s40101-015-0060-8

40. Mashrita Naure Cloud. (n.d.). *29 Best air purifying plants from NASA clean air study.* Retrieved April 10, 2020, from https://www.mashrita.com/29-best-air-purifying-plants-nasa-clean-air-study/

41. National Center for Complementary and Integrative Health. (n.d.). *Aloe vera.* Retrieved April 10, 2021, from https://www.nccih.nih.gov/health/aloe-vera

ACKNOWLEDGMENTS

So many people have contributed their time and support to this book. While I don't have enough space to thank all of you, know that you are truly loved and appreciated for the value you have brought to this book project and my life's journey. To that end, I'd like to individually acknowledge the following people for their role in this journey:

Terri Eileen Liggins, author, writer, serial entrepreneur, rawtarian, friend, mentor: Terri, who would have thought that meeting you during a vision board workshop would change my life in so many ways? As if your background weren't impressive enough, your talent, creativity, and drive continue to amaze me with each passing day. I'm eternally grateful to call you a mentor, colleague, and friend. Thank you for encouraging me and showing me another way to make my dreams come true.

Frank Hyman, writer, mentor, friend, savvy entrepreneur: I was on the fence about attending my first-ever conference for authors in 2014. Even though I had yet to write a book or begin making a name for myself as a writer, you saw past all that and immediately took me under your wing. Thank you for encouraging me to ignore the little stuff, get out of my own way, and go for gold.

Lori DeMilto, writer, mentor: I appreciate you for teaching me the value of persistence and diligence in our industry. Without question or judgment, you were one of the first people to take me under your wing when I made this leap into medical writing eight years ago. You've been there every step of the way, and I hope to pay it forward.

Tara Haelle, journalist, writer, colleague phenom: You've been a part of my journey as a professional writer and journalist almost from the very beginning. From serving as a mentor during a science writing fellowship to challenging my thoughts, Tara, I thank you. Even though you are always insanely busy and globe-trotting, you have made time for me between trips to drop gems that I continue to carry.

Jill Rendelstein Fulmer, editor, writing coach, Wonder Woman of Home and Office Life: After eight years of working on this book project with no visible end in sight, finding you was the best decision I ever made to finish this book. I appreciate your objectivity and editorial services. Without you, I'd still be sitting at a coffee shop writing additional pages instead of acknowledgements!

Dr. Devona Williams, colleague, entrepreneur, visionary, spiritual big sister, devoted mother and wife: As you know, being the unintentional new kid on the block was a challenge, but you were there to support and encourage me every step of the way whether it be work, spirituality, charity, or just life in general. Thank you for your knowledge, wisdom, humility, grace, and kindness.

Dr. Donney John, colleague, mentor, influencer: Thank you for your candor and encouragement to go the extra mile even during those times when I thought I'd run out of gas. I'm honored to have you as part of my network and look forward to watching your start continue to rise as you embark upon the next chapter in your contributions to the world.

Derik Hicks, copyeditor: Thank you for copyediting this book. I believe that everything happens for a reason, and how we initially connected was no accident. Although our relationship is fairly new, you've already taught me so much about patience, objectivity, and of course, the value of candid feedback.

Johnny Turner III, proofreader: Johnny, I cannot thank you enough for your diligence in proofreading this book. It was a process, but you hit it out of the park. I appreciate you being a part of my journey and giving me honest feedback.

Janine Bolon, unflappable entrepreneurial juggernaut and overall bad-you-know-what: Connecting with you was one of the most positive aspects of the COVID-19 pandemic. As our relationship evolves, you continued to amaze me with your resourcefulness, innovative thinking, efficiency, leadership, and sense of charity. Thank you for inspiring me and always challenging me to reach higher.

Dr. Tam Nguyen-Cao: I'm honored to have you as a friend and appreciate your support and encouragement more than you will ever know. I look forward to continuing to follow your greatness.

Dr. Frieda Wiley, PharmD, is a licensed pharmacist, medical writer, and journalist who writes for pharmaceutical and biotech companies, universities, associations, and other organizations. Her work has appeared in *O, The Oprah Magazine*, WebMD, publications by the National Institutes of Health, and many more. A free spirit at heart, the Texas native and digital nomad calls home wherever her spirit is called for the next adventure.